The Campus Community Confronts Sexual Assault

Institutional Issues and Campus Awareness

Edited by Juneau Mahan Gary

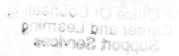

ISBN 1-55691-113-0

Learning Publications, Inc.
5351 Gulf Drive
P.O. Box 1338
Holmes Beach, FL 34218-1338

Printing: 5 4 3 2 1   Year: 8 7 6 5 4

Printed in the United States of America.

CONTRIBUTORS

Marta Aizenman, Ph.D., Director, Counseling Center, Cook College, Rutgers-The State University of New Jersey, New Brunswick, NJ

Carol Andrews, M.A., Author, *Avoiding Rape On and Off Campus*, Pitman, NJ

William David Burns, M.A., former Assistant Vice President, Student Life Policy and Services, Rutgers-The State University of New Jersey, New Brunswick, NJ

Karen Calabria-Briskin, M.A., former Program Specialist, NJ Division on Women, Trenton, NJ

Carol Evangelisto, M.A., Counselor, Psychological Counseling Services, Trenton State College, Trenton, NJ

RoseMarie Fassbender, R.N., M.A., former Director, Health Services, Trenton State College, Trenton, NJ

Juneau Mahan Gary, Psy.D., Director, Psychological Counseling Services and Coordinator, Sexual Assault Victim Education and Support (SAVES) Program, Trenton State College, Trenton, NJ

David Jenkins, M.D., former Physician, Health Services, Trenton State College, Trenton, NJ

Susan E. Karr, D.A., former Director, Office for Women, Trenton State College, Trenton, NJ

Georgette Kelley, Ed.D., Director, Psychological Services, Douglass College, Rutgers-The State University of New Jersey, New Brunswick, NJ

William Klepper, Ph.D., Dean, Student Life, Trenton State College, Trenton, NJ

Robert McCormack, Jr., Ph.D., Assistant Professor, Department of Law and Justice, Trenton State College, Trenton, NJ

Philip Witt, Ph.D., former Director, Psychology Department, Adult Diagnostic and Treatment Center, NJ Department of Corrections, Rahway, NJ

ADVISORY BOARD MEMBERSHIP

Beth Amoroso, B.A., Victim/Survivor, Trenton, NJ

Rosalie Pataro, M.A., Adjunct Instructor, Department of English, Trenton State College, Trenton, NJ

Mary Taylor, M.A., former Coordinator, Rape Care Program, NJ State Department of Health, Trenton, NJ

CONTENTS

PREFACE

Sexual assault on campus is not a new phenomenon or recent crisis. Behaviors resulting in date or acquaintance rape have occurred on campuses for decades. There are at least three differences between campuses of past decades and campuses of the present: (1) attitudes about male and female roles and responsibilities have changed; (2) a term, "date rape" or "acquaintance rape," is now attached to the behavior; and (3) society is reframing perceptions of responsibility and blame for this behavior and is moving from "he just took advantage of me" to "date rape" and from "why were you wearing that skimpy outfit?" to "he violated you."

The crisis of date rape occurred in the past but no one knew that a response was necessary, and no one knew how to respond nor where to seek help. Consequently, laws and campus judicial procedures are now reflecting contemporary thought. Social, medical and legal services exist on many campuses and in the surrounding communities. The changing contemporary views of date rape and sexual assault are further hastened by the Campus Awareness and Security Act (Public Law 102-325) which requires each campus to provide education/prevention programs and intervention/therapeutic services.

This book is designed to help colleges and universities cope with sexual assault and its effects. A campus unprepared to cope with a sexual assault can *contribute to* the victim's trauma and create legal problems. This book is a comprehensive and practical resource which will help colleges and universities avoid such problems and improve current services. The chapters encompass the significant sexual assault issues and concerns of institutions of higher education, including assessing the problem; instituting policies, procedures, guidelines and support programs; establishing education and prevention programs; encouraging faculty involvement; and developing staff training. The emphasis is on *practical* suggestions, programs, policies, guidelines and procedures to prevent sexual assault and to handle a sexual assault effectively.

The chapters cover the full spectrum of sexual assault concerns, appealing to residence hall staff, administrators, campus organizations, counselors, campus police, clergy, health personnel, faculty and students.

ACKNOWLEDGEMENTS

This book was made possible by several people to whom I am grateful. Special thanks are extended to the Advisory Board Members for their insightful comments and suggestions. Acknowledgement is extended to William Klepper, Dean of Student Life, Trenton State College, and to the college administration for their support of this project. Gratitude is given to Cheryl Green, the Rev. Wayne Griffith, the Rev. Joseph Halpin, Rabbi Howard Hersch and Kathleen Keresey for their comments on specific chapters. Appreciation is given to Karen Haftl, Helen DiMaggio, Mae Chester-Hall, Faith Pennant and Sandra Whaley for their clerical assistance, to Barbara M. Green for her assistance and to June Narod for her graphics skills.

On a personal note, I thank my family (the Mahan, Foushee and Gary-Pugh families) for instilling and reinforcing in me the qualities of optimism, perseverance and compassion. Finally, and most importantly, many thanks and much love to my husband Mel who has supported and encouraged me and has spent many, many hours alone without complaint as I completed this book.

AN OVERVIEW OF SEXUAL ASSAULT ON CAMPUS

by Juneau Mahan Gary

No campus is immune from sexual assaults. They occur on campuses located in suburban, rural and urban areas; at private and public colleges; at ivy league, city and state universities; and at two-year and community colleges. In fact, the incidence of sexual assault, and crime in general, has been increasing on campus. "Whether this is an actual increase in the number of abusive, assaultive and harassing incidents or one of improved reporting procedures is of secondary importance to the reality that such behaviors leave scars" (Roark, 1985, p. 15).

Sexual assault, in the most general sense, is unwanted and non-consensual sexual contact, including stranger and date rape or attempted rape. Date rape is the most prevalent type of sexual assault on campus, occurring when the offender (such as a classmate, friend, lover or study partner) is known to the victim, and when sexual contact is perpetrated against her will.

A startling conclusion reached by Koss, Gidycz and Wisniewski (1987) is that 53.7 percent of female college students who responded to their survey revealed some form of sexual victimization, and that 25.1 percent of male college students admitted to engaging in some form of sexual aggression. "Virtually none of these victims or perpetrators had been involved in the criminal justice system; their experience would not be reflected in official crime statistics" (Koss et al., 1987, p. 168). Similarly, Byington and Keeter's (1988) survey revealed that one-third of the respondents had been a victim of some form of sexual assault and that 48 percent knew a victim.

Other studies also support the notion that the incidence of date rape is greatly under-reported and remains a significant but rarely visible problem on campus. A typical naive comment is "it wasn't rape, he just took advantage of me" (Parrot, 1988, p. 1). Furthermore, most victims do not use campus services such as counseling, health services and campus police, in seeking help. When they do seek help, they tend to do so during the crisis phase, and only seven percent of the victims talked to a counselor about being assaulted. On the other hand, 80 percent of victims disclosed to their friends and 37 percent confided in their relatives that they suffered sexual threat or battery (Koss, 1987).

Women between the ages of 16 and 24 years, the age range of the traditional college student, are at highest risk for sexual assault, according to the FBI. First year women, in particular, are vulnerable because they are in transition from the structured environment of home and high school to increased freedom on campus and have not developed skills to balance independence and personal safety. Furthermore, the campus culture is such that many male students traditionally perceive first year women as vulnerable and naive.

The threat or fear of a sexual assault by a stranger can be serious enough to adversely alter a woman's lifestyle. Some female students who fear being assaulted by a stranger restrict their regular activities and limit their ability to pursue an education, especially during the evening and early morning hours between 5 p.m. and 5 a.m. A quote taken from the Project on the Status and Education of Women (1985, p. 3) makes this point: "I feel unsafe on campus at night. I never take classes with finals scheduled at night. Unfortunately, several classes were required and I have to wait until next year to take them."

While some female students feel restricted by the threat of sexual assault, others feel a false sense of safety while residing on campus. A residence hall director recalled encountering a female student jogging alone on a suburban campus at 2 a.m. When asked why she was jogging alone at such an hour, her reply was, "It's okay, I'm on campus." Her naive response implied that a fellow student would not attack her and that an off-campus offender would be dissuaded from entering the campus.

Whether an assault was perpetrated by an acquaintance, mate or stranger, it is well documented that alcohol consumption by the victim or offender is involved in 50 percent or more of the sexual assault cases (Benson, Charlton and Goodhart, 1992; Abbey, 1991). Alcohol abuse reduces the sense of personal responsibility, reduces inhibitions and decreases judgment for the victim and the offender. Among students, it is of special concern because the offender can more easily gain sexual control of the victim by entrapping her (i.e., getting her drunk). When a victim drinks, it reduces her ability to disengage or to defend herself, and it reduces the likelihood of positively identifying the offender. It also decreases the likelihood that her objections would be believed by the offender and others. When the offender drinks, it reduces his judgment and sense of personal responsibility. His lack of good judgment allows him to engage in behaviors which he may have avoided when not under the influence of alcohol. As he walks away from the incident, he feels less responsible and makes statements such as ''I was too drunk to remember my actions.''

Reducing sexual assault on campus should not be limited to what women should or should not do for self-protection. This traditional focus places undue burden on women, implicitly communicates the condoning of inappropriate behaviors for men and combats only **half** of the problem. Reducing sexual assault will not be effective unless some programs are focused on potential offenders, who are almost exclusively men. Scant attention is traditionally given to prevention awareness programs focusing on **men** as potential offenders. Most men are not likely to change their behaviors, values and attitudes until they examine and label them as aggressive and violent.

Increasing the campus community's awareness of sexual assault for women **and** men involves the cooperation and commitment of concerned students, influential faculty and key administrators. In the experience of many sexual assault experts, such cooperation and commitment develop as a *reaction to* assaults rather than as a proactive and preventive response *before* assaults occur.

Each campus community must ask its members the following types of questions: Is the physical, emotional and financial trauma experienced by victims pervasive enough to eliminate the risk of sexual assault? Would the institution's reputation be adversely affected if sexual assaults occur on this campus? Would this institution be liable if an assault occurred on campus?

WHAT CAN WE DO?

The Campus Awareness and Security Act (Public Law 102-325) (NASPA, 1993) was designed to promote the prevention of sexual assault, to improve services for victims and to clarify sanctions for offenders. It now requires each campus community to provide educational/prevention programs, intervention/therapeutic services and training for its students, staff and faculty. The Act makes otherwise voluntary programs and services at self-selected campuses a requirement for **all** campuses. In addition to the requirements of the Act, the campus community can take individual and group responsibility for reducing sexual assaults on campus. No community member should say that the problem is too overwhelming for the individual to make a significant contribution. The following proactive measures represent interventions ranging from personal changes to institutional changes. Some of the most important changes require little or no expenditure of funds.

Interventions Requiring Little or No Cost

- Develop a campus policy for sexual assault and design quidelines to educate the community and to assist victims. Disseminate the information.

- Encourage the campus community to use common sense for personal safety.

- Sponsor a Sexual Assault Awareness Day, Week or Month. April is the official awareness month sponsored by the National Coalition Against Sexual Assault (NCASA).

- Sponsor a "Take Back the Night" Program.

- Encourage the faculty to incorporate sexual assault issues into the curriculum. (For example, an English professor can assign novels or short stories about sexual assault or literature written by a victim (e.g., Maya Angelou).

- Write letters to the editors of the campus and municipal newspapers and to local, state and federal legislators to increase awareness and advocate for better services and funding.

- Involve the faculty in developing field placements with sexual assault programs. With some degree of creativity, this can be accomplished for students in several academic majors.

- Distribute a "Sexual Assault Guarantee" (Benson, 1992).

Interventions Requiring Some Financial Cost

- Bear in mind that as you read this list, the financial costs of instituting such measures should always be balanced against the human and financial costs of not doing them. Logic and sound management dictate that the interests of all are best served by adopting such positive and proactive steps.

- Compile a resource library composed of videos, films, books and pamphlets for training, classroom and personal use.

- Design and regularly offer a course such as "Contemporary Issues," to focus on sexual assault and other problems such as racism, sexism, eating disorders, substance abuse, suicide, physical disabilities and sexual orientation.

- Install state-of-the-art security systems which are "user friendly" and which deter illegal entry.

- Develop a comprehensive sexual assault program designed to educate the campus community and assist victims.

- Hire a coordinator or director of sexual assault prevention services.

- Establish a hotline and an escort service for evening hours.

- Develop advocacy, counseling and support services; train trainers; develop a speaker's bureau; create a victim accompaniment program; develop on-campus and off-campus referrals; locate referral services for offenders; disseminate educational and printed resources; and establish victim support groups.

- Develop a peer educator program to facilitate awareness programs.

Distribute a list of interventions similar to the ones mentioned above which everyone can either participate in or initiate. Two strategies will help to make this project successful. First, arrange projects in three categories: "for women," "for men," and "for everyone," so no one can say "I don't have to do anything because I'm not a member of that group." Further, these categories reinforce that **everyone** can and should do something to prevent and combat sexual assault. (See *Appendix A* for an example of interventions). Second, include items which can be accomplished by individuals (e.g., maintain a bulletin board about sexual assault issues) as well as by groups. This strategy encourages individual responsibility and action so that the student feels a sense of accomplishment without feeling overwhelmed. Projects requiring group participation can be overwhelming and they relinquish individual responsibility to the point of believing that others will lead the project.

Peer Educators. A peer education program is a low budget mechanism to make a broad spectrum impact on campus. The literature supports the use of peer educators in their ability to be effective in modeling and influencing positive peer behavior (Bylington & Keeter, 1988). Until recently, peer educators were an untapped resource on campus. These students can be volunteers or can receive stipends, academic credit or student aid funds. With proper training in group facilitation and supervision, a small group of mature student-peer educators can make a significant impact in educating other students about sexual assault in freshman seminar classes, in residence halls, in academic classes, for student organizations, for athletic teams and for other special gatherings on campus such as fall orientation programs. The greatest individual change usually results from intimate discussion groups and self-exploration. The inclusion of **men** as peer educators is a significantly strong aspect of a peer educator program for two reasons: (a) studies have indicated that male discussion groups led by men are usually effective because men talk more openly to each other than in mixed-gender groups (Beneke, 1983; Egidio & Robertson, 1981; Lee, 1987) and (b) male participation emphasizes that sexual assault affects everyone and they are part of the solution. Male groups allow men to evaluate male behaviors such as sexual stereotyping and aggression in dating situations as well as in their values and attitudes about women, violence and sexuality. If men re-think their attitudes and behavior, they may develop increased insight, experience less denial and change their behaviors.

The use of male peer educators for sexual assault is relatively unique because men are seldom involved in the preventive education of rape and seldom employed as sexual assault peer educators. Male peer educators are the primary tool in reaching other men, who are typically the offenders.

Using the male peer educators for male groups has not been employed widely and may be effective in assisting to make significant changes in their perceptions of sexual assault.

Training for peer educators should emphasize presentation/facilitation skills and technical information through videotaped role plays and mock sessions. While female peer educators should be relatively easy to recruit, male peer educators, however, would require specific recruitment strategies, such as personal invitations to men with an interest in preventing sexual assault, men who sought counseling to help their partners who were victims, or male sexual assault victims (confidentiality would be maintained).

CONCLUSION

Sexual assault is an under-reported and serious issue on campus and is finally getting recognition through the Campus Awareness and Security Act. A proactive and reasoned response appears to be the most effective mechanism in coping with and preventing assaults. Each campus should develop a mechanism to educate all students, faculty and staff about the impact of sexual violence, ways to prevent assaults and ways to assist assault survivors.

ADDITIONAL RESOURCES

Organizations

National Coalition Against Sexual Assault (NCASA)
2428 Ontario Rd., NW
Washington, DC 20009
(202) 483-7165

Center for the Study and Prevention of Campus Violence
Towson State University
Administration Bldg. #110
Towson, MD 21204
(410) 830-2178
(Sponsors the "National Conference on Campus Violence")

Network of Victim Assistance (NOVA)
1757 Park Rd., NW
Washington, DC 20010
(202) 232-6682

Books and Journals

Rape . . . Awareness, Education, Prevention and Response: A Practical Guide for College and University Administrators, 1992, D. Keller.

Crime on Campus: Analyzing and Managing the Increasing Risk of Institutional Liability, 1991, P. Burling.

Acquaintance Rape and Sexual Assault Prevention Training Manual, 1988, A. Parrot.

Sexual Assault and Child Sexual Assault: A National Directory of Victim/Survivor Services and Prevention Programs, 1989, L. Webster (Ed.). (Includes state agencies, national organizations and agency profiles).

Sexual Assault on Campus: What Colleges Can Do, 1988, A. Adams and G. Abarbanel.

The State-by-State Guide to Women's Legal Rights, 1987, N.O.W./Legal Defense and Education Fund and R. Cherow-O'Leary.

Rape Intervention Resource Manual, 1977, P. Mills (Ed).

Journal of American College Health, "Violence on Campus: The Changing Face of College Health" (Special Issue), January, 1992, 40(4).

Journal of American College Health, "Research Perspectives on Campus Violence" (Special Issue), January, 1993, 41(4).

Helplines

Sexual Assault Support Service • (800) 788-4727

Self-Help Clearing House • (201) 625-7101 (in NJ) or (800) 367-6274. Provides information on support groups and offers free consultations on how to start new support groups.

Victim/Witness Hotline call (800) 555-1212 and ask for a telephone number for a specific state. Provides financial assistance to victims and witnesses of violent crimes for expenses related to medical, emotional and funeral fees and loss of wages.

DEVELOPING A CAMPUS-BASED SEXUAL ASSAULT PROGRAM

by Susan E. Karr & Juneau Mahan Gary

The history of a social movement can often be traced through its names. "Women's suffrage," for example, became "women's liberation," and ultimately "the feminist movement." Likewise, where once people talked about "rape," today they speak of "sexual assault" or, more politically, "violence against women." Such changes in nomenclature are more than cosmetic; they reflect fundamental changes in attitudes toward and management of an issue.

To illustrate, consider the history of Trenton State College's response to the problem of violence against women on its campus. What began in 1979 with the Coalition of Women Against Rape, evolved into the Sexual Assault Victim Education and Support Unit (SAVES-U). This chapter will review the evolution of this case illustration and will conclude with recommendations for developing an effective campus-based sexual assault program.

ADMINISTRATIVE CONCERNS

What questions might administrators ask themselves when considering the development of a campus-based sexual assault program? Trenton State College's experience in creating a program produced a number of key questions.

1. Why are we considering a sexual assault response and education program at this time?

CHAPTER 2

2. Who initiated the idea of developing a program?

3. Who is supportive and who is likely to resist this program? What groups, constituencies or power positions do they represent?

4. How will such support or resistance shape the program?

5. Do we have the necessary expertise on campus to develop and staff a program?

6. What resources are we willing to commit to this program? For how long?

7. Where will the program be located administratively and physically? Why?

8. What will the program's relationship be to the campus and local police, health services, women's center, counseling services and the college administration?

9. What is the mission of the program? Will it be educational, referral, direct service, or a combination? Why?

10. What community resources exist to support this program?

11. What credentials should be required of the program's director and support staff?

12. Should the staff include volunteers?

13. What kind of evaluation process is needed for program development?

14. How will the program impact on the college's liability?

TRENTON STATE COLLEGE: CONTEXT AND PROGRAM

Trenton State College is not, on the surface at least, different from most colleges. However, in the late 1970's, among its returning women students and female faculty and staff, there was a small group of activists who expressed dissatisfaction with a range of issues affecting women. In 1970's activist fashion, these women formed a grass-roots coalition and developed a proposal creating a new campus office: the Office for Women. The proposal was approved and the first director was hired in 1978. She facilitated the formation of the Coalition of Women Against Rape, consisting primarily of returning women students active with the campus Women's Center.

The Coalition's task took on added urgency following two sexual assaults and one attempted sexual assault within a six-month period in 1979. The Coalition requested the formation of a crisis group and advocated staff training in education and prevention programs. These programs coincided with the distribution and analysis of a questionnaire on campus safety conducted by the faculty union. In response, the administration convened a Rape Task Force and charged it with developing a campus communication and services network for sexual assault victims. The Task Force was composed of a cross-section of the campus community. It included representation from offices that a victim might contact following an assault. The primary focus of the task force was on the medical and psychosocial needs of victims following an assault, rather than on prevention and education activities for the entire campus.

The Program. The Rape Task Force recommended the establishment of a rape support program to be coordinated by the Office for Women. The support program would be staffed 24 hours, 7 days per week by campus volunteers, and linked by two beepers and an on-campus hotline.

In 1980 the program was approved and the first volunteer support persons were recruited and trained. A group of eleven women faculty, staff and students emerged and served in pairs (with one member carrying the beeper) for two week periods. A hotline was established with its own telephone number; it rang at the Health Center and Campus Police Department where 24 hour assistance was available. Rosters with volunteers' telephone numbers were kept in both locations and either office could contact the support person. The volunteers' names remained concealed from the general campus community so that victim privacy could be maintained in case the victim and support person were seen in public together.

The program was publicized so that if a victim sought help for a sexual assault from any campus office, a staff person would inform her about the rape support team. If a victim called the hotline directly, a volunteer would meet her and assist her in contacting the necessary offices and agencies for help.

Recruitment, training, evaluation and other aspects of volunteer management took far more time than anyone had anticipated. In addition, the rape support program operated on a minimal budget of $1,230 (which has not increased in ten years). Three quarters of the budget covered beeper rentals and training expenses; the remaining portion covered miscellaneous expenses. Other institutional expenses, such as telephone and postage, were absorbed by the college.

Within three months of operation, the word "assault" was added to the program to broaden its responsibility. The Rape Hotline became the Assault Hotline and included rape, sexual assault and physical assault. The importance of this shift cannot be overemphasized. In broadening its language, and consequently its thinking, the program and the institution moved towards an understanding that sexual violence involved much more than rape. Volunteers and others soon realized that sexual violence has many victims: roommates, relatives and significant others who also need support, along with the primary victims.

In its second year, the most controversial aspect of the volunteer program was the inclusion of men as support persons. Initially, there was concern and uneasiness about including male volunteers as supporters of female victims. One objection was that a male would not be able to accompany a female victim during certain medical procedures. Furthermore, some believed that a female victim might feel uncomfortable talking with anyone except another woman about the assault. As a result, the controversy was resolved by using men as volunteers for male victims and for male friends and relatives of female victims.

An important contribution came from a male faculty member, who indicated that the program's name, "Rape Support Team," suggested support *for* the act of rape rather than for its victims. Consequently, the program's name was changed to "Rape Victim Support Team" to accurately reflect its mission and services for victims.

As the program matured, prevention and educational services were deemed to be essential components of a comprehensive program. Significant policy issues, including the following, had to be confronted:

1. Who is responsible for keeping records? What kind of records should be maintained? What information should be recorded?

2. What does "confidential" really mean?

3. Who should have access to the records? Under what circumstances should information be released?

4. What does the college do when the victim is a minor?

5. Who has the authority to contact parents?

6. When and how should parents be contacted?

7. Whose insurance covers an accident during the transportation of the victim for medical assistance by a volunteer using his/her own vehicle?

8. What kind of selection and training methods are best in working with volunteers?

9. Who has the authority to investigate a charge of rape?

The Stepchild. The Office for Women was eliminated in 1982. As a result, the sexual assault program no longer had a permanent base or coordinator. It became a "stepchild" and resided with whomever would accept it. Those who tended to accept it, did so for personal interest and out of a sense of commitment. When each successive coordinator left the college, the program became a stepchild again and needed to be "adopted" by another coordinator. No long range plans were considered by administrators to give the program organizational permanency and priority until 1987.

The program was co-coordinated briefly by two Student Life staff members. They changed the program's name to SAVES-U the (Sexual Assault Victim Education and Support Unit) to communicate a broader scope of services, including education. It also made services available to victims of incest, acquaintance rape and sexual harassment who might previously have excluded themselves from seeking services. The coordinators also developed relationships off campus, seeking legitimacy through associations with other recognized groups such as the New Jersey Coalition Against Sexual Assault and the county sexual assault program. The coordinators received a small service grant to sponsor a training conference for colleges and universities located in the county.

In spite of these successes, co-coordination was abandoned as unworkable after one year, and SAVES-U moved under the domain of one coordinator. When this coordinator left the college, SAVES-U moved to the Counseling Services and a revitalization of the program was unsuccessfully attempted. Another revitalization was attempted by a different coordinator the following year; it, too, was of limited success. Operating funds for the program which remained in another office, were shifted to the SAVES-U coordinator so that consistency between leadership and resources could be a reality. Currently, the program has a coordinator and a small group of volunteers, now called peer educators, who focus on educational services solely. The program relies on services available through the county sexual assault program for victim support, crisis counseling and emergency medical assistance.

LESSONS LEARNED

Administrative Structure. The difficulties in establishing a viable assault prevention and intervention program at Trenton State College offer valuable lessons for other campuses. One lesson is the importance of creating and funding a staff position to direct the program. This person should have expertise in sexual assault issues. Lacking such a person, Trenton State had to proceed by trial and error. The "growing pains" felt by the institution and by the individuals involved were difficult and emotionally draining; obvious errors perceived by some were usually sincere efforts by others.

Another lesson is the importance of an appropriate organizational structure for the program. The placement of SAVES-U with an individual rather than with an *office* produced constant turnover in coordinators. This, in turn, produced short-term, erratic, crisis-oriented programming. While the program was a priority for the Office for Women, once the office was closed, the program became just one of several responsibilities for a series of coordinators. The lesson is that continuity is imperative for a program to succeed.

Volunteers and Peer Educators. One of the program's major weaknesses (and one not unknown to most volunteer organizations) has been difficulty in recruiting and retaining volunteers and peer educators. Among the explanations for this are: lack of recognition or acknowledgment by the administration; anonymity brought about by the need for confidentiality for those who assist victims; emotional fatigue or burnout; attracting the small group of emotionally mature and responsible peer educators who can educate others about sexual assault; and retaining peer educators whose first priority is academic course work and who have interests in other equally important campus projects and activities. The stress of being personally, professionally and emotionally prepared to assist a victim or educate others, while fulfilling professional duties, academic requirements and personal responsibilities, has remained a significant issue, and one that defies easy answers. Some volunteers have felt less prepared to help a victim than others in spite of regularly scheduled training sessions; this also contributes to turnover. Peer educators are trained each semester and are instructed to educate solely and refer those needing assistance. (Strategies for volunteer management and retention are addressed in *Chapter 5.)*

Another problem, one that has become particularly acute in the last few years, is apathy. Many members of the campus community do not perceive sexual violence to be a problem on campus and consequently do not feel a vested interest in addressing the problem. Ironically, this lack of interest is occurring during a period of open and honest discussions in the media about date rape and other forms of sexual assault. Those who volunteer to assist now usually have personal motivation in that they had been a victim of sexual assault or knew a victim.

PROGRAM DEVELOPMENT

Perhaps the most important lesson is that program development should follow four basic steps: assessment, planning, implementation and evaluation. These steps should improve the chances of instituting an effective program. Adams and Abarbanel (1988), Mills (1977), Parrot (1988, 1991) and Warner (1980) are excellent resources for further detail. The four steps are described below:

I. Assessment

- Create a credible committee, composed of a cross-section of the campus community. Representation should be balanced, broad and limited to no more than about twelve members. Membership should include: (a) students; (b) faculty; (c) administrators and staff responsible for providing services to victims (such as counselors, police, nurses, clergy, residence hall directors); (d) women's, minority and gay organizations; (e) advisors to the Greek organizations; (f) the administration's legal advisor; and (g) community organizations (such as the local sexual assault program and the county prosecutor). The committee should be appointed by an executive officer and report to the same.

- Agree on an operational definition of sexual assault.

- Identify the nature of the problem on campus.

- Conduct a *needs assessment*.

a) Collect data on reported, unreported and attempted sexual assaults on campus. Include the FBI, state and local crime reports.

b) Collect information on how the institution has responded (or not responded) to student reports of assault.

c) With the support of the campus office of Institutional Research, develop a questionnaire or survey on perceptions about sexual assault. Distribute the survey to students, faculty and staff. Analyze the results.

d) Using counselors or trained volunteers, interview primary and secondary victims who are willing to discuss their experience.

e) Using counselors and trained volunteers, interview those on and off campus in a position to help, such as campus police, counselors, residence hall directors, the judicial officer, the county prosecutor, local women's shelters and support programs and hospital administrators. Mills (1977) offers a list of pertinent questions to ask.

f) Evaluate the physical environment for needed improvements on campus (e.g., lighting, security doors, etc.).

■ Conduct an *environmental scan* to determine and understand the culture of the institution, the surrounding community and the state. Analyze and incorporate the results in the program planning and development.

a) Review current and past issues of the student newspaper and the college catalog to develop a profile of the student body, as well as the non-academic emphasis of the institution.

b) Study speeches and other official college documents to understand administrative priorities.

c) Obtain copies of relevant state statutes and pending legislation regarding sexual assault, HIV, and abortion in cases of rape and incest.

d) Review current and past issues of local newspapers to understand political and cultural environment, forces, and trends.

e) Conduct discussions with campus and community leaders. Analyze the information and interpret the strategic importance of issues and trends.

f) As necessary, develop issue papers for use in program planning.

■ Identify assault-related problems for the institution (e.g., a decrease in student enrollments, negative publicity) and barriers to resolving the problems.

■ Identify incentives for the institution (such as prevention of future assaults, victim support) to support the program.

■ Identify supportive administrators and those who potentially will resist the program.

II. Planning

A plan is a method or program to accomplish a clear set of goals. The assessment process should be used to design a program based on the needs, characteristics and funding limits of the institution.

■ Develop strategies to overcome pivotal problems, barriers and disincentives (e.g., offer academic credit or a small stipend to attract and retain student volunteers and peer educators).

■ Pursue adequate funding on campus.

■ Pursue public and private grant funds.

■ Develop goals, objectives and strategies based on expected accomplishments (e.g., schedule a meeting with the Inter-Greek Council to arrange a series of assault awareness programs for its members).

■ Specify time lines within the confines of the academic calendar.

■ Visit other campus sexual assault programs to determine their strengths and weaknesses.

■ Determine legal and liability issues and questions, such as the following:

a) Will the institution's liability insurance cover the sexual assault program?

b) In what ways, if any, will a written policy statement increase or decrease the institution's liability?

c) How will assault survivors who are minors be handled? Under what circumstances, will parents be notified? Must parents sign a consent form for the college to take specific actions?

d) How will dissatisfaction by the victim or accused be handled to discourage a civil or criminal law suit?

e) What legal and financial responsibility, if any, will the institution assume for assault cases?

f) How will a court subpoena be handled?

g) How will confidentiality be handled? What professions have privileged communication? What are the legal limits of, and restrictions to, confidential material? Should the victim's professors be informed, especially if class time will be missed? Where will written information be kept?

h) What are the liability issues involved in giving advice to victims, including victims who are minors?

i) How should inquiries by the campus and local media be handled? Who should be the spokesperson? What type of information should be divulged, if any?

j) How should mistakes be handled to avoid a civil or criminal law suit?

k) When should other campus offices become involved, either with or without the victim's knowledge, when their area of expertise becomes necessary (e.g., a victim threatens suicide)?

l) How should disclosures of illegal activity be handled? Will the program be perceived as sanctioning illegal acts or divulging information to authorities?

m) What role should the institution play in taking disciplinary action against those charged with sexual assault.

n) How should off-campus assaults be handled?

Clearly, this list could continue indefinitely in a litigious atmosphere, such as currently exists. These types of questions and others should be answered prior to implementing the program. It is important, therefore, that the campus attorney be consulted during program planning.

- Develop an approved policy statement on sexual assault which involves a cross-section of the campus community. It should include the following:

a) Legal and other definitions of sexual assault;

b) Types of sexual assault;

c) A review of the law and examples of unacceptable behavior;

d) A review of campus and community judicial procedures and consequences for assailants in sexual assault cases; and

e) Identification of campus resources for support and assistance for victims.

- Develop a policy dissemination plan to include distribution to students (undergraduate and graduate), faculty and staff.

- Decide on the type and scope of the program to implement. Will it be available to students, faculty and staff? Will it include victim support, advocacy and education? Will it offer hotline and walk-in services, follow-up care, speaker's bureau, escort services, 24 hour services? Will services be offered for the offender? Will it use paid staff, volunteers, or a combination?

III. Implementation

- Hire or appoint a coordinator.

- Publicize the program (e.g., campus newspaper, flyers, etc.)

- Distribute written guidelines to the following offices: health center, campus police, counseling center, residence life.

■ Distribute written guidelines to the following offices for confronting the alleged offender: residence life, judicial officer, campus police.

■ Develop strong relationships with other offices and programs which can provide expertise for training or for victim support.

Such offices may include campus police, health center, counseling centers and specific faculty.

■ Implement a recruitment plan. Include discussion about field experiences and academic credit for student volunteers and peer educators.

■ Implement an effective training program (i.e., one that combines initial, intensive training with follow-up).

■ Develop a plan to strengthen campus security by remedying the physical inadequacies of the campus as identified in the assessment process.

Identify community agencies for possible referrals.

■ Contact off-campus agencies and identify ways to effect change, such as legal reform or political action, at the local, state and national levels. Organizations such as the following should be good places to begin: the state's Division on Women, Office for Rape Care, local rape crisis programs, the National Coalition Against Sexual Assault (NCASA) the National Organization for Women (N.O.W.), and the National Organization for Victim Assistance (NOVA).

■ Identify community funding sources which are consonant with the institution's philosophy, if campus funding is inadequate.

IV. Evaluation

■ Conduct periodic evaluations to assess staff and volunteer performance, victim satisfaction, interaction with the campus community and interaction with the local community.

■ Publish a year-end report with statistics, accomplishments and areas in need of improvement.

CONCLUSION

Trenton State College's decision in the late 1970's to develop a formal response to sexual violence on campus was necessitated by the campus self-admitted unpreparedness in the face of a series of violent assaults. The college viewed the problem as serious enough to warrant attention. Other colleges and universities planning to implement a campus-based sexual assault program may be able to avoid the mistakes and benefit from the successes of this program.

CRIME PREVENTION: ROLE OF THE CAMPUS SECURITY GROUP

by Robert J. McCormack & William M. Klepper

In April, 1986, a 19-year-old freshman at Lehigh University in Easton, Pennsylvania, was raped, robbed and murdered as she slept in her residence hall room. She was murdered by a fellow student who lived off campus. The latch on an exterior door was propped open, apparently by another student, to facilitate an after-curfew return.

The vicious nature of the attack shook campuses across the country and raised serious questions about the ability of campus security forces to protect students from such random and unpredictable events. It underscored the fact that there was little information available about the nature and number of violent crimes occurring on campuses. Further, the incident raised questions about the legal responsibility of the institution to disclose information to parents and prospective students about the serious nature of crimes on campus.

The parents of the Lehigh University victim, Connie and Howard Clery, received a negligence settlement from the University. They established a clearinghouse called "Security on Campus." It provides information on campus crime and security measures and is a lobbying group to heighten public awareness about crime on campuses. Their initiative resulted in a 1988 state law in Pennsylvania requiring colleges and universities to make available their data on crime and security problems to parents and prospective students on request. In 1990, the national "Crime Awareness and Campus Security Act" was passed by the United States Congress and is now law (PL 102-325). Initiated by the Clerys, it requires virtually all colleges and universities to provide, upon request, accurate statistics on all homicides, rapes, assaults, robberies and burglaries on their campus for the three previous years, as well as provide sexual assault prevention programs and intervention services for victims.

The Lehigh University case and other brutal campus crimes in recent years have made campus security a major issue for administrators. It seems that the civil liability of institutions in connection with acts of violent crime may be a catalyst for developing comprehensive crime reporting and crime prevention techniques.

MEASURING CRIME ON CAMPUS

Under what circumstances is an assault likely to occur? Are incidents of sexual assault becoming more frequent? Who is likely to be the offender? These and other important questions need to be answered if we are to determine the causes of assaults and ways to prevent them.

Recent studies addressing campus sexual assault indicate that it is a common problem. A frequently cited study at Texas A&M University assessed the incidence and risk factors for date rape and other forms of male-against-female sexual aggression. It indicated that 77% of the women and 57.3% of the men had been involved in some form of sexual aggression, and that 14.7% of the women and 7.1% of the men had been involved in unwanted intercourse (Muehlhard & Linton, 1987). Another study of 7,000 students in 35 colleges and universities in the United States found that one woman in eight had been raped, according to the legal definition, in the year previous to the survey, and only 10% of them reported it; ninety percent knew their assailants, and 47% of the rapes were by first dates or romantic acquaintances. One out of 12 men in the study admitted to having fulfilled the prevailing definition of rape, yet none identified himself as a rapist (Koss, 1982).

Only about 10% of the nation's 3,000 colleges and universities submitted crime statistics voluntarily to the FBI prior to PL 102-325 (O'Reilly, 1990). Now that colleges must report crime statistics, we can expect the data to improve. Because reliable data were not available until recently, it is difficult to determine whether the incidence of sexual violence on campus is on the increase or simply receiving long overdue attention.

CAMPUS SECURITY RESPONSE

Campus security is an administrative responsibility which is usually delegated to campus police and residence hall supervisory staff (referred to here as the campus security group). The campus security group is guided by established intervention strategies and uses highly structured discretion when confronted with curfew violations, underage drinking in residence halls, traffic violations and other violations. Serious criminal complaints such as sexual assaults require a more complex and coordinated response, often involving municipal law enforcement officials. Because of the traumatic nature of these offenses and the equally traumatic impact of the decision to report the incidents, total victim support and criminal prosecution are necessary if such crimes are to be reduced.

Providing security on campus is a difficult task that differs substantially from that of local law enforcement. The unique nature of the campus clientele, coupled with a mandate to maintain high levels of security and supervision while assuring broad access and privacy, produces a complicated situation (Burling, 1991). For example, maintaining perimeter security is difficult to provide in view of the administration's desire to be accessible to the community. Overly restrictive regulation of access tends to develop a fortress-like perception of the institution that is seen as counterproductive for effective community relations. Residential supervision is further complicated by changing mores regarding casual sex among consenting adults. It is also complicated by easy access to alcohol which is available at many student gatherings. Thus, it is difficult to determine where institutional responsibility for student interaction ends and student-to-student privacy begins.

Traditionally, institutions develop policies governing conduct and judicial procedures to handle violations for student, faculty and staff. This information is usually disseminated in student and faculty/staff handbooks. They indicate in detail, the elements of proscribed behavior, the procedure by which charges will be brought and the penalty for sustained charges. Student cases are delegated to a campus judicial officer and disciplinary board for processing. It is noteworthy that an institution's student conduct code, including grounds for dismissal, need not be as limited and rigorous as criminal codes.

A sexual assault is usually defined as a serious criminal complaint. Such complaints should be reported to municipal police for arrest and prosecution. Criticism by students regarding administrative attempts to adjudicate these complaints on campus are on the rise. Recent cases at Carleton College in Minnesota, ("Lawsuit Charges Mishandling of Rape Cases," New York Times, 1991a), at the College of William and Mary in Virginia, ("Students Date-Rape Complaint Jolts William and Mary: Criticism of Administration's Reaction Has Campus Confronting Difficult Issues," *Washington Post,* 1991), and Stanford University in California, ("Task Force Seeks Revised Handling of Rape Charges," *New York Times,* 1991b), are cases in point. A staff member at the College of William and Mary said, "The most shocking thing is they, (college officials) don't see it (date rape) as a violent crime. They're treating it like it was some kind of misunderstanding."

Lodging criminal charges in domestic violence incidents tends to result in a reduction of such incidents (Steinman, 1987) because formal processing sends a clear and unmistakable message that such conduct will *not* be tolerated. One would expect the same to be true for sexual assault.

CAMPUS SECURITY/POLICE

The Campus Police Department is generally responsible for two major crime-related tasks; preventing crime and reducing the fear of crime. Crime prevention in its broadest sense involves anticipating criminal acts and "target hardening" (i.e., raising the difficulty level to successfully commit a crime). Reducing fear of crime involves techniques and strategies to provide a sense of heightened security and personal safety.

Crime Prevention

Crime prevention strategies usually include two specific tasks: (1) monitoring and regulating access to campus grounds (usually at a gate), facilities and events; and (2) developing crime-specific patrol strategies to thwart potential offenders. For campuses with a well-defined perimeter and limited access, effective monitoring may present no serious obstacle. Campus patrols, parking permits and identification cards tend to discourage trespassers. However, controlling access for many urban campuses may not be a realistic objective in light of less clearly defined boundaries, public thoroughfares through campus and a strong reliance on public transportation by students, faculty and staff.

One alternative is for urban campuses to develop prevention strategies based on the analysis of crime statistics. This may include placing officers in high incident areas on the days and at the times those incidents are likely to occur. Under urban conditions, maintaining a close liaison with municipal police agencies is vital because they represent increased resources. For example, a program utilizing the University of California at Berkeley Police Department and City of Berkeley Police Department yielded dramatic results in crime reduction. The combined forces patrolling the campus perimeter and area immediately surrounding the campus resulted in over 1,000 drug and weapons arrests, a 40 percent reduction in violent crimes, and a reduction in stranger rapes from seven in 1986 to zero in 1988 (Hodge & Blyskal, 1989).

A comprehensive crime prevention inventory can assist in identifying security inadequacies on any type of campus. It includes a review of eleven areas and each is discussed below:

1. **Facility Design and Security.** Little can be done to change facility locations or original building designs. However, the combination of several physical changes can result in a significant increase in security. Consider the following suggestions: improve interior lighting; install security mirrors in elevators; and restrict access from ground floor windows. In the residence halls, install the following: security peepholes in every door, electronically secured exits (to avoid "propped open" doors), computer-controlled access to residence halls activated by each student's identification card, a 24-hour/year round security alarm system for live-in staff which is connected to the campus police dispatcher and tamper-resistant screening on ground floor windows. Additionally, establish procedures for a residence hall lock change if a room key is lost, and develop a residence hall security check point for evening and weekend hours. Finally, changing pedestrian traffic patterns, removing obtrusive shrubbery and strategically locating emergency ("blue light") telephones can result in increased security.

2. **Site/Exterior Lighting.** Adequate exterior lighting should receive high priority. A good test for adequate lighting is the existence of at least one well-lit and convenient pedestrian route, with "blue light" phones, between any two facilities on campus.

3. **Key Control.** Clear procedures should be implemented for issuing keys, recording their possession and enforcing individual accountability for access to academic buildings and residence halls. One office should be responsible for periodic key inventory, re-keying and enforcement procedures.

4. **Access Policy, Controls and Community Relations.** Establish an access policy that carefully balances community relations with the safety of the campus community. The relationship between the college and the community is a major factor in the crime prevention equation. Efforts should be made to involve community leaders and interested citizens in the internal affairs of the institution and to have them view the institution as a vital resource for their community. Community interest programs and special education programs to address specific community needs should be provided. Close relationships between the college community and neighborhood residents will tend to reduce crime and vandalism on campus grounds. They should also demonstrate a willingness to get involved in a cooperative effort with the community to confront crime and criminals on the campus perimeter. In the final analysis, policies encouraging strong campus-community relationships are most effective in improving campus security.

On many urban campuses, trespassers commit most of the violent crimes. Intruders should be apprehended if a law is violated and remanded to the municipal police for prosecution.

If further illegal behavior occurs by the same trespasser, campus police should take immediate enforcement action rather than wait for an incident to occur. Crime prevention should be a two-way street: campus and municipal police should work cooperatively to confront crime and criminals.

5. **Alcohol Policy and Enforcement.** Intoxication has a positive correlation to one's likelihood of committing an offense. It also has a profound influence on one's vulnerability to victimization. In both instances it impairs one's judgment and reduces one's inhibitions. Students under the influence of alcohol are particularly vulnerable as offenders and victims of stranger and date rape. The alcohol policies should be consistent with municipal and state laws and should be enforced. Outreach

should be made with the local business community to ensure that the sale of alcohol is made in strict compliance with existing laws. Student education programs sponsored jointly by the administration and student organizations should address the dangers of immoderate use of alcohol. Policies restricting the possession or use of alcoholic beverages in public and private areas on campus should be part of the orientation for all students at the beginning of each semester and enforced by the campus security group.

6. **Anti-Hazing Policy and Enforcement.** Deaths and sexual assaults in connection with fraternity and sorority events necessitate a university policy to regulate Greek-letter hazing activities. This standard should also apply to other social events, even though they may not be affiliated with the Greek system. Clear rules and penalties should be articulated and incorporated into the new member orientation process. A campus advisor to the Greek-letter organizations should be appointed or hired to function as the campus liaison with the national offices. Further, this advisor should be responsible for monitoring activities, enforcing policies and planning educational programs.

7. **Campus Disciplinary and Judicial System.** This system confronts students accused of being in violation of campus standards of conduct. In general, an activity which threatens the welfare of others or the campus community is subject to sanction. Criminal acts such as physical assault, theft, drug possession or use, unlawful entry and disorderly conduct may result in arrest by campus police. Student handbooks should address, in detail, issues of expected and proscribed student conduct and due process policies relative to the student judicial structure. Disciplinary procedures which are clearly articulated and objectively enforced, represent an effective mechanism for social control and for removal of individuals who pose a threat to the campus community. The implementation of disciplinary policies, however, should be subject to periodic review to determine their effectiveness.

8. **Educational Programs.** Prevention programs designed to increase awareness about crime (and sexual assault) are important. At least one police officer or other safety expert

should be trained in crime prevention tactics and regularly speak to groups, highlighting how students may unintentionally contribute to crime (e.g., propping exterior doors open) and orienting students to campus security procedures. This should be part of the new student orientation program and reinforced each year. The issue of self-defense, especially as it relates to sexual assault, should be addressed. The most common forms of resistance according to national victim surveys include fighting back physically, acting non-violently but trying to escape, and screaming to frighten the offender and attract help. The advantages and disadvantages of these and other possible self-defense strategies should be presented and discussed. Innovative programs such as the Sexual Harassment and Rape Prevention (SHARP) program at the University of New Hampshire and Individuals Concerned About Rape Everywhere (ICARE) program at Lehigh University should be encouraged and supported by administrators. The SHARP program features weekly meetings in residence halls to discuss rape and to develop healthy relationships between men and women. The ICARE program encourages students to develop videos in which a date turns into a date rape and the incident is discussed. Arranging site visits to exemplary campus sexual assault programs in your geographic region would be a good way to evaluate the strengths and weaknesses of your program in comparison to another program and to seek support to strengthen your program. Administrators could be instrumental in consulting with the academic departments to include sexual assault issues in academic courses. This could be accomplished by encouraging term papers, debate issues and speeches about sexual assault issues and field placements at sexual assault programs.

Administrators should also organize an annual "Sexual Assault Awareness Week" and identify a group, such as the student government association, to sponsor or co-sponsor it. A proactive and consistent awareness program can have a dramatic effect on sexual assault reduction.

9. **Patrol Procedures, Police Staffing and Training.** Conspicuous patrols at specific times and places using foot patrols or the "park-walk-and-talk" concept seem to be most effective. This concept requires the motorized officer to leave

the vehicle when not on assignment, then patrol on foot in the proximity of the vehicle, until called to another assignment. While on foot, communication is maintained by a portable radio. This procedure provides many of the benefits of foot patrol while providing a rapid response to emergencies. For small campuses, the use of golf carts and bicycles for security personnel should be explored. One Canadian municipality uses bicycles successfully for routine patrols. Bicycle patrol allows the police officer access to tight areas or areas off limits to motorized vehicles. Communication is maintained by a portable radio.

Issues of security staff retention and training should be addressed. Frequently, remuneration is not competitive with municipal police and attrition may be significant. Training issues should focus on technical competency (such as correct procedures for evidence collection), as well as on human factors demonstrating sensitivity to the victim (such as the officer's mannerisms, attitude and use of non-technical language).

Student assistance for crime prevention should be used where feasible. Student assistants supplement the campus security system by providing additional eyes and ears. Students can be used in a student watch program, as campus escorts at night and as security personnel in residence halls. A screening process and sufficient training for students are necessary for them to understand their purpose and limits and to know when to request professional intervention.

10. **Enforcement Philosophies and Practices.** Campus enforcement policies and practices should be reviewed by the campus security group and the administration periodically. A basic commitment to fair, consistent and objective enforcement should be maintained.

In cases of serious crime, such as sexual assaults, offenders should be remanded to the municipal police for prosecution. Rule violations and minor offenses by students may be referred to the campus judicial office. Criminal or disorderly behavior by trespassers may require action ranging from arrest to expulsion from campus.

11. **Administrative Coordination and Communications.** Two-way communication should exist between the campus police and the administration. Operational procedures and official communication channels should be established to report serious crimes or unusual occurrences on campus. Off campus, procedures should be established for gathering and reporting campus crime statistics in compliance with the laws governing such reporting. Finally, campus police should be represented on committees related to security and quality of life issues.

RESIDENCE LIFE SUPERVISION

Competent, consistent and responsive supervision in the residence halls is a major source of social control for students living on campus. Most students respect the guidance and discipline offered by residence hall directors in an environment where the unbridled freedom of a few may impinge on the safety and well being of the majority. The residence hall staff is usually a combination of administrative professionals and mature students, many of whom are trained in crisis intervention. They are usually the first to arrive at the scene of potentially criminal or disruptive incidents in residence halls. If not already trained, they should receive extensive training in crisis intervention and referral, including special instructions for assisting sexual assault victims and the impact of post-traumatic stress disorders. Training should focus on what the residence life staff should do if they are the first contact with the victim following the assault. The staff should be aware that any statements or records are subject to subpoena and records should be accurate and complete. The staff may be required to testify in court. Additionally, residence life staff will be involved in the campus judicial process if the offender is identified and is a student.

CONCLUSION

There is no guarantee that sexual assault in particular, and crime in general, will not occur on a campus which has instituted the guidelines outlined in this chapter. As much as one would like to think otherwise, crime and violence seem to be a part of the reality of campus life. As with other dangers of contemporary living, safety on campus requires lifestyle accommodations and common sense precautions. Yet one thing is certain: failure to plan effectively for the possibility of sexual assault will only make matters worse for students whose rights are violated and for fear generalized on campus and in the surrounding community.

MEETING RECOVERY NEEDS OF VICTIMS

by RoseMarie Fassbender, David Jenkins,
Robert McCormack & Carol Evangelisto

The sexual assault victim may experience difficulty in seeking help, or the appropriate type of help, to assist her in recovering from the physical and emotional trauma. This chapter addresses how campus staff can effectively help the assault survivor.

SAFETY FIRST

Sexual assault constitutes a health and safety risk. Therefore, the first concern of each campus following an assault is to ensure the health and safety of the victim. Her physical well-being and the initiation of emergency medical treatment, if necessary, should be the immediate objective. The second concern is for the proper and timely collection of evidence in the event that she files legal charges.

If the victim calls the campus police emergency number, health center or sexual assault hotline, the responder, using a calm and reassuring voice, needs to determine the victim's location and telephone number (if possible). The helper should keep her on the telephone, if possible, until help arrives. If she can get to a safe location without much additional trauma, suggest she do so. If she is at a safe location already, suggest that she remain there until *identified* police, ambulance, residence staff, nursing staff or sexual assault support personnel arrive. Before disengaging the telephone call, the responder should have a clear understanding of where she is and where she will be met. This information is vital in case help arrives at the safe place and the victim is not there. If there is some miscommunication, the helper can check the

CHAPTER 4

victim's intended path in case she was unable or too frightened to move from the original location or if she became immobile or unconscious along the way.

Enhancing Coping Skills. The sexual assault victim has experienced a significant stressor and her coping resources will most likely be challenged significantly. The responder should acknowledge the psychological trauma and assist in a calm, reassuring and nonjudgmental way to encourage a trusting relationship and to remind her that the environment is now safe. Offer her choices, unless she is so distraught that this is not advisable. Attempt to re-establish a level of functioning at least equal to, if not better than, the pre-crisis level. In this way, the anxiety will usually not escalate to panic. If the client is in a state of panic, the following actions should prove useful:

1. Remain with her; leaving her alone may increase feelings of isolation and panic.

2. Maintain a calm and reassuring manner.

3. Allow her to cry or ventilate feelings and thoughts. Active listening combined with realistic options provide an atmosphere that tends to reduce anxiety.

4. Use short, simple sentences with a firm voice to convey that someone is in command of the situation.

5. Keep environmental stimuli to a minimum. A quiet and relaxed environment, incorporating soothing colors, sounds, lighting and scents, is preferable. Restricting the number of people in the immediate area reduces noise and distraction.

6. Wait until the victim has regained composure before asking questions.

Emotional responses of victims will vary depending on their usual coping styles and other circumstances such as whether the attacker was a stranger or acquaintance, the degree of force used and the degree of physical injury. Some victims appear calm and controlled; others do not. Their range of reactions can include *fear* (the primary reaction of most women), *anger* (directed at the offender, police officer, medical staff or legal system), *tension* (sometimes expressed as a paradoxical smile), *composure* (from shock or the need to project an external appearance of strength) and *crying* (from emotional and physical pain). The reactions are known as the "rape trauma syndrome" and are explained in detail in Burgess and Holmstrom (1979). It is important for the responder to recognize the wide range of possible reactions that may occur, and not be fooled by an outward appearance of calmness or be angered by a seemingly inappropriate and hostile outburst.

The helper needs to be available in whatever capacity necessary, according to the needs of the victim. Additionally, helpers must be aware of their own anxiety level. If the helper is anxious, the victim will usually sense it. Excessive or insensitive comments may be detrimental to the victim's sense of well-being.

REPORTING A SEXUAL ASSAULT

The trauma of sexual assault will have a significant influence on the victim's decision to proceed with a formal complaint and subsequent medical examination. Conditions which adversely influence a victim's decision to file a complaint include the following: fear of retaliation; fear of police, hospital and court procedures; fear of parental anger; fear of not being believed; feelings of embarrassment and self-blame; concern for an adverse reaction of a jealous boyfriend or husband directed at the victim or the offender; and a lack of faith in the justice system.

A support person can follow the steps below to ensure the best possibility of successful prosecution, once the victim's physical safety has been established and she has been informed of the steps. Individual judgment and discretion are advised:

1. Inform someone about the incident as soon as possible.

2. Seek a mature person, such as a trained volunteer, who will remain with her and support her during the initial stages of the reporting process and subsequent medical examinations.

3. Request a medical examination if it has not been arranged.

4. If the victim decides to press charges, she should insist that a report be taken and that it be checked for accuracy.

5. Help her to compile a list of the names of pre- and post-incident witnesses; that is, people who saw her with the offender before or after the incident.

6. Assist her in making a statement to the prosecutor regarding the incident, particularly detailing the elements of the crime as specified in the state's penal code. Also, she may choose to file a complaint with the campus judicial officer and may need support.

Public Disclosure and Confidentiality. Which of the victim's statements become part of the public record and which remain confidential? If the crime of sexual assault is reported in a residence hall, then the residence staff is usually required to follow a set of standard operating procedures developed by the institution. Interviews with the victim, witnesses and offender (if still present) are recorded as official documents and an "incident report" is filed. These and subsequent follow-up reports by administrative staff are public documents subject to court subpoena. Reports taken by campus police or municipal police are likewise subject to presentation in court. Medical records indicating the results of *emergency medical evaluation* and *treatment* following the assault are subject to subpoena if the prosecutor decides to pursue the case. Non-emergency medical records remain confidential and cannot be released without the written consent of the individual.

In the event that the victim seeks professional or pastoral counseling, these records are confidential, as are conversations between the victim and the attorney. Testimony of the victim's sexual history is not admissible in most jurisdictions; rape shield laws protect victims in this regard.

REFERRING THE VICTIM FOR TREATMENT

Although the victim should be encouraged to seek medical attention, she often hopes the problem will "just go away." Avoiding medical assistance, is common, especially when it means many personal questions will be asked. Painful events must be re-explored and the victim's body, which has already been injured and violated, will be inspected and examined.

The victim's initial reaction, especially if it is a date rape, is often "I'm not going to prosecute so why be examined?" She may change her mind about prosecution at a later time, so by seeking medical attention immediately, she improves the chances of a successful prosecution and can document the assault with medical evidence. What is of greater importance, though, is that medical attention will assure that the obvious injuries and not-so-obvious internal injuries are treated. Taking such action demonstrates to the victim, her family and her friends, the serious nature and reality of the trauma. An explanation of what the medical examination will entail, and advice regarding the right to ask questions, is information that the responder can share with the victim.

If the victim is transported to the hospital by ambulance, the ambulance crew should be aware of protecting the physical evidence and providing emotional support. If such training is not evident, it is important that campus staff advise the ambulance crew of the safeguards to protect the evidence and appropriate interventions to decrease the victim's anxiety.

The health center staff or campus police should know which hospital is approved to perform an evaluation and treatment for sexual assault victims. Many states now have specially trained personnel at hospitals who examine the victim, collect specimens according to legally rigorous evidence collection methodology and treat the victim. Encourage her to make decisions (when possible) and ask if she wants an accompaniment (e.g., friend, significant other, support person, female officer) to the hospital. Call the hospital in advance to inform them of a referral and provide preliminary information; this should speed their reaction time. The health center staff should have follow-up contact to offer her emotional support or other referrals.

The purpose of the physical examination is to gather evidence for possible prosecution and to provide emergency treatment. The physician does not determine if a sexual assault has occurred; the court makes this determination.

The hospital personnel will document their findings. The examination will be followed by a medical interview once she is determined to be physically stable and in no danger of complications. The interview consists of: (1) the reconstruction of the assault; (2) gynecological history; and (3) general medical history. The thorough, objective and precisely written medical record and interview will be the victim's best source of evidence in court or at the campus judicial hearing.

The medical record may be significant in refreshing her memory in preparation for the trial. Such information and detail may be difficult to recall unless she was interviewed immediately following the medical examination and able to refer to it prior to the trial or hearing. Prior to discharge, the medical staff will discuss options for handling pregnancy, HIV infection, and sexually transmitted diseases (STDs). She should be given written discharge instructions because her memory may not be clear or she may be in a state of shock. She needs to be apprised of symptoms which might develop in the following days and should be given important telephone numbers for the attending physician and sexual assault crisis center.

If days or weeks have elapsed since the assault, the purpose of the physical examination will be to identify and treat injuries or STDs which may have resulted from the assault. A pregnancy test may be ordered. It is also important to assess if referral for additional services is required. Aggressive anal intercourse can produce breaks and tears in the mucous membranes of the anus. Such breaks in the membrane increase the likelihood of an exchange of infected body fluids. Immediate and follow-up testing for HIV is advised.

Victim's Rights. Encourage the victim to ask questions and help her to understand her rights. According to Johnson (1985), victims have the right to:

1. Ask if there is a separate waiting room and examination room for sexual assault victims. The separation tends to decrease the discomfort of waiting among strangers when she may be wearing torn clothing or may be partially disrobed. Moreover, a separate area usually reduces generalized anxiety to strangers, especially to men, who could evoke unpleasant memories of the assault based on an appearance, scent or innocent gesture.

2. Have someone accompany her through the examination process. In New Jersey, for example, the hospital staff is required to inform her about counselors who will accompany and assist her.

3. Request the presence of a female police officer if one must be present during the examination.

4. Request that if photographs must be taken, that a female officer, nurse or physician do so. Photographs may strengthen the evidence against the offender, but the victim has the right to refuse being photographed.

5. Refuse to have her name given to the news media; she should advise the hospital personnel of this request upon admission. The news media usually respects the victim's anonymity.

6. Request that irrelevant information which may damage her credibility (e.g., previous treatment for drug or alcohol abuse) not be divulged.

7. Change her mind and refuse treatment and leave the hospital at any time. She also has the right to inquire about the medical and legal consequences of treatment.

EMOTIONAL IMPACT AND COUNSELING

Each victim's emotional reaction is not predictable. Generally, the long term emotional adjustment following an assault requires much more work than is initially apparent. The victim must attempt to resolve issues of fear, anger, humiliation, gossip, control, self-esteem, privacy and the like while continuing academic studies. Usually her grades drop. Often her intimate relationships suffer. A referral to counseling can assist her through the long term recovery process.

The campus counseling center and local or campus sexual assault program should prove helpful. The counselor should be able to intervene (with a signed consent form) to request or arrange, for example, a change in residence hall assignment, reduction in course load or granting of an "incomplete" grade. Off campus, the counselor may be able to intervene by contacting the violent crimes compensation board for unreimbursed expenses related to the assault. In most states, either the prosecutor's office or violent crimes compensation board usually assist with out-of-pocket expenses.

Grief. When someone has lost something of value, the universal reaction to the emotional pain of that loss is grief. Sexual assault victims have lost many things of value; among them might be innocence, virginity, belief in the world or the goodness of people, pride, physical well-being, security, freedom, trust, self-image, routine, plans, friends, partners, sexual desire and a belief in themselves and their ability to judge others. Grieving (also called mourning) is the process of dealing with and healing from the pain of such losses.

Theorists vary on the absolute number of stages in the grief process. Kubler-Ross (1969) uses five stages while others, such as Tatelbaum (1980), use three stages to describe the grief process. The point is that the stages are a practical application for understanding the grief process.

Following a sexual assault, a reactive grieving process begins. A reactive grief process is different from an anticipatory grief process in that the latter occurs when the loss is expected but has not yet occurred, as in a terminal illness. The reactive grief process, as used by Tatelbaum (1980), involves three identifiable stages (which can best be described as (1) the shock or numbness stage, (2) the suffering or disorganizational stage and (3) the recovery stage. Each stage is described below.

The *shock stage* is characterized by feelings of disbelief, unreality and a numbness that insulates the victim from feeling the full impact of her loss. This may be confusing to those around her who may wonder why she is not crying uncontrollably, or how she is able to continue functioning and attending to the details of her life.

Her sadness is usually pronounced. At times, the numbness may mask her sadness, but it does not mask her anger which may seem irrational and uncontrollable when she inappropriately lashes out at others. Like her sadness, it too is very real. These reactions need to be anticipated and accepted as a normal part of the healing process.

As the insulating effect of the numbness gradually begins to wear off, the victim begins to feel the full emotional impact of the assault, and the second stage of grieving, the *disorganization stage* begins. Surges of contrasting emotions wax and wane, leaving the victim confused and exhausted. She may feel totally despondent, collapsing into long bouts of sobbing one moment and recoiling into a stoic trance the next. She may feel helpless to stop the flood of thoughts about the details of the attack and yet find her mind going blank when asked to recall something as simple as her own license plate number. She may insist that she wants to be left alone one day and feel overcome with a need to be listened to, talked to, touched, held or taken care of the next. Additionally, feelings of helplessness, hopelessness, vulnerability, anger, bitterness, guilt and self-pity come and go with no predictable pattern. Severe anxiety, accompanied by a host of symptoms including dream disturbances, auditory and visual flashbacks of the attack, dizziness, trembling, body aches, heart palpitations, shortness of breath, irritability, insomnia, decreased appetite and related weight loss are also a normal dimension of this stage. Depression, too, must also be considered a normal response in the suffering stage. However, because depression can rapidly progress to a more severe state in which suicide becomes a clear threat, helpers must be prepared to recognize any significant changes and immediately refer the victim to a counselor for evaluation.

Finally, it must be mentioned that in the disorganized or suffering stage of grief, the victim may spend a great deal of time asking herself "Why me?" Again, this is a normal part of grieving. However, if this question becomes a way for the victim to continuously blame and punish herself, then referral to a counselor or clergy would be appropriate and helpful.

With the passage of time and the support to others, the victim will begin to notice longer periods of time when she is free of the intrusive thoughts about and feelings related to the attack. She will begin to focus on her future again and continue to find ways to incorporate the attack and its emotional and physical consequences into her life experience. When she begins to do this, and to notice that she is doing it, then the *recovery stage* has begun. This does not mean she is fully recovered, rather, it indicates her emotional readiness and willingness to reclaim her life. Helpers must be prepared to recognize this stage and to champion her cause as she takes her first meager step forward. They must also be willing to support her when she falls backward, which she will, and frequently, at first.

Aftershocks are an important phenomenon to be recognized in the recovery stage. These are the unexpected reminders of the attack (such as the scent of a cologne), or the losses attached to it, and the brief setbacks that they cause. The victim can easily and quickly recover from these setbacks without losing her focus on her present or future functioning.

Having now reviewed the three stages of grief as they relate to sexual assault, a few other important points must be made.

    a)   Though it is important for a victim to pass through each of the stages to fully recover, this passage may not be a smooth progression from one stage to the next. More likely progressive/regressive movements will occur and eventually subside when the victim is able to incorporate (not forget) what has occurred and when the emotional pain, while not forgotten, is no longer the intense, disruptive experience it once was for her.

b) The duration of the grieving process is unique for every victim depending on what other stressors pre-existed the assault and what coping skills were used.

c) There is the possibility that a victim can get "stuck" in one of the first two stages. Counseling is usually effective in assisting a victim's progress through the stages.

Why me?   *Why did this happen to me?*
(or Why did this happen to her?)

What did I do to deserve this?
(or What did she do to deserve this?)

Why do bad things happen to good people?

Why is God punishing me?
(or Why is God punishing her?)

Questions similar to these are usually asked by victims and their secondary victims such as friends, family, lovers and roommates. A student may ask these questions of a minister or rabbi, residence director, physician, counselor, police officer, Dean of Students or secondary victim. Campus clergy, staff and administrators may be challenged to assist a victim in ways which, perhaps, surpass their formal area of expertise. As they grapple with these questions, it is important that they do so in ways that will not contribute to the victim's feelings of guilt.

Many assault victims raise questions about goodness, kindness and fairness in life and may question the existence and intentions of God or a spiritual being. Feelings of self-doubt and anger toward a spiritual being may be evident. This type of spiritual and psychic burden, in addition to the trauma of sexual assault, can place an unfair and complicated challenge before the victim or secondary victims. Additionally, she may feel the need to seek absolution and to "cleanse the soul" in an attempt to feel clean and whole. The need for absolution may suggest her confusion about her role in the assault and the limits of the unrealistic expectations of her responsibility to thwart it.

Krauss and Goldfischer (1988) and Kushner (1981) devote entire books to the question of why bad things happen to good people. These short books can be read as an adjunct to philosophical and religious discussions or counseling sessions by those questioning a spiritual meaning. These books suggest that the question "why me" is pointless and keeps the victim glued to the past. Rather, they advise that victims can confront the past by looking into the present and asking "now that this has happened to me, what am I going to do about it?", instead of asking "why did this happen to me and what did I do to deserve this?" The message here is clear: encourage her to live in the *present* and to *take control* of her life. Living in the *past* closes off exits, leaving her feeling trapped with an undue burden, while living in the *future* can develop into a preoccupation with fears and worries which give her no rest and encourage paranoid paralysis. The helper's task, therefore, is to help her remain in the present and focus her energies on changing and influencing things within her control.

During a crisis, the listener should not take the victim's questions of "why me" literally and embark on a logical, theological or philosophical discussion. Instead, respond to the victim's hurt; use empathy, reflection and active listening; seek clarification; and attempt to share or experience the victim's emotions. Once the victim feels accepted, she may be able to discuss deep and troubling feelings that she could not discuss with others. It is important for the listener to remain based in reality and not try to "make nice" and repeat trite expressions like "be strong" or "everything will be fine," when both of you know differently but neither will acknowledge it. The victim needs to feel "yes, I'm understood," although it may not be expressed verbally.

Is there an answer to why bad things happen to good people? No. The listener should attempt to refocus her to the present and on what to do *now*, and not on why did it happen to me?

FIELD EXPERIENCE: CREATING A WIN-WIN SITUATION

by Juneau Mahan Gary

News casts of current events during the past year showed people helping people . . . We witnessed people from all over the country and from all walks of life rush to help the victims of hurricanes and to rebuild south-central Los Angeles after the riots. We witnessed President Carter and his volunteers rebuild houses through Habitat for Humanity. During spring break, professors escorted groups of students to depressed areas such as Appalachia, to assist with legal issues, income tax preparation, rebuilding homes and feeding the hungry

People helping people is not a new concept. The concept of helping others needs improved packaging for the 1990's. New terms such as community service and internship/field placement are attracting the attention of students as they seek ways to combine volunteerism with academic requirements.

Undergraduate and graduate students represent a tremendous potential source of help for sexual assault programs, and a resource which is seriously undertapped. Most campus sexual assault programs, however, are too underfunded for the staff to devote serious attention to developing a quality field placement experience for students. Such an undertaking requires significant time and investment to recruit, train and use students effectively.

Yet a field experience teaches students valuable skills while they can earn academic credit in a "hands-on," supervised environment. Such training should not be confused with volunteer help for routine and drudgery tasks. Instead, field experience is a mechanism to supplement current staffing needs, while also teaching valuable skills to students. The

CHAPTER 5

student can use this experience as a stepping stone to a career, while at the same time helping those in crisis. A field experience can include an internship, independent study, cooperative education arrangement and practicum. It is sanctioned by an academic department and receives academic credit.

If sexual assault programs invest in student training, then the campus can strengthen its relationship with community agencies through field placements. In considering these field placements, sexual assault programs off campus tend to offer four types of experiences of relevance to students: counseling, hotline/crisis intervention, prevention and advocacy. *Counseling and hotline intervention* will tend to attract those students primarily planning to enter the helping professions, such as counseling, social work and psychology majors. Undergraduates should probably be limited in their counseling responsibilities in sexual assault programs off campus. The typical undergraduate may not be objective or experienced enough to handle demanding issues. *Advocacy projects* will most likely attract students who want to "change the system," such as criminal justice and women's studies majors. *Prevention activities* usually attract students from all majors.

STUDENT FIELD PLACEMENTS

Student Assessment. Career counselors and professors should help each student to determine needs and objectives in pursuing a field placement. The following questions are useful:

- How will a field placement improve your class performance?

- What skills do you want to develop and why?

- What skills and interests do you bring to the field placement?

- Are you seeking personal contact with victims or do you prefer non-victim contact?

- Do you want to explore a variety of career fields or is your career interest clear?

- What are your career goals and how will a sexual assault placement assist you in reaching your goal?

- What do you hope to gain from this placement?

Placement Selection. The student's needs should be matched with the program's needs so that maximum learning and placement satisfaction will result. Encourage investigation of the program's philosophy of service, mission statement and type of clients served to determine if the placement is consistent with the student's expectations. Obvious factors such as time requirements, transportation needs and out-of-pocket expenses should be considered. Academic concerns such as relevance, type and breadth of experience, and number of credits attempted, must also be considered.

Undergraduates. Help to establish personal and professional limits before beginning a placement. Most students begin a placement with much idealism, energy, commitment and enthusiasm. However, they have not had the life experiences to understand emotional exhaustion connected with counseling and advocacy in the sexual assault field. This is not to imply that such a placement should be avoided. To the contrary, it can be very rewarding when a victim is helped or when the student observes the persistence, resourcefulness and accomplishments of the staff constrained by limited resources.

Students must understand beforehand that they may not be able to enter an agency to "counsel" victims in the way that a trained professional counselor might do. Instead, they should use the placement to develop skills congruent with their personal life experiences, academic level and theoretical knowledge.

Undergraduates are well-suited for activities requiring advocacy, educational workshops, "linking" tasks which help victims through a transition period and special projects (such as using art skills to develop brochures). They can expect to gain skills in public speaking, referral, basic listening and crisis intervention while also observing the criminal justice and social service systems. Their time also should be used to observe the functions of different positions, both paid and voluntary, with the goal of learning how each person developed the skills necessary for the position and how the position contributes to the program's mission and purpose.

Graduate Students. Students with one or several placements are able to improve their academic performance by integrating theory and skills and analyzing the results in class. With the completion of a placement, they often are hired immediately when they enter the professional job market. Most agencies prefer to hire someone with experience; the field placement is an excellent mechanism to develop professional expertise.

Advanced students can expect to develop counseling, crisis intervention, public speaking, advocacy and administrative skills. Counseling will probably begin with specially selected victims or with co-counseling or co-intake arrangements.

Male Students. Male students also should be encouraged to pursue field placements in the sexual assault field. Such placements may demand creativity and flexibility in identifying appropriate assignments and experiences. Sexual assault affects everyone, and men are as much a part of the solution as are women. By virtue of their placement in an agency, they can provide a valuable service by serving as a model of appropriate male behavior.

AGENCY ISSUES IN FIELD PLACEMENT

Financial Support. Campus programs often do not take into account direct and indirect costs in developing a reputable field placement, even when students work without pay. Direct costs such as postage, telephone, training materials, travel allowance, office supplies, insurance and awards for recognition may add up proportionally for each student. Indirect costs such as supervision, management and extra clerical demands, lighting, heating and office space can be overwhelming for a fledgling program. Also, graduate students tend to "cost more" because their academic programs set requirements with which a field placement must comply. For example, a graduate student fulfilling a counseling placement needs a private office for confidential counseling and crisis intervention. Thus, a realistic review of the agency's present and potential financial resources is necessary to make an informed decision to become a field placement setting.

Administration Preparation. The program should establish a firm field placement foundation prior to recruitment. Such a foundation should:

- Seek the support of administrators and paid staff. Include them in the recruitment, training, supervision and evaluation of field placements.

- Determine placement objectives and length of placement (i.e., one semester, summer only, academic year or a combination).

- Develop an orientation and pre-service training program and a field placement handbook. Decide on the type and structure for interviews and the selection criteria for applicants.

- Establish a marketing plan with the career counseling office (or individual responsible for developing field placements) and with someone who can assist in facilitating the recruitment.

- Develop a procedure for regular contact with agency representatives regarding students in field placement.

- Talk to the career counselor, academic chairperson and individual professors about the types and lengths of field placements a student can pursue through your program. Ask them about procedures to talk directly to students in classes, in clubs (e.g., Psychology Club) and on residence hall floors. Place ads in the school newspaper and on the campus radio and television stations which inform students about what your program can offer.

Recruitment. A well-planned and well-executed recruitment plan is essential. Keep in mind the academic calendar and plan to recruit at least one month prior to academic registration, which necessitates recruitment to occur one semester prior to the placement. This strategy allows students time to evaluate placement sites and decide to register for a placement. Most institutions register in March/April for the fall semester and in October/November for the spring semester. Call the registrar or academic department for dates specific to an institution.

Because the sexual assault field may carry a stigma and is not perceived as glamorous or well-paid, the personal touch is often necessary to recruit top students. Short presentations made in targeted courses, with the professor's approval, are helpful. Another entree into the classroom is to offer to lecture on sexual assault for a specific course. Before concluding, make a short announcement about the placement and distribute the brochures.

Selection. Interview students to match their needs with the program's objectives. Send a letter of agreement to the student with a copy to the field placement coordinator.

Orientation and Training. Orientation enables students to be thoroughly acquainted with the program. Distribute a reading list, if required, well in advance of the starting date. A large block of time (i.e., full day or several days) allows for team building and skill enhancement in a supportive environment. Include the secretary, staff and executive director of the agency. A tour of the building provides a visual and spatial perspective. Distribute a calendar of training dates and topics. A suggested forty hour training program is presented in *Appendix B.*

Supervision and Evaluation. A basic requirement for field placements is supervision by approved staff members. Individual or group supervision affords the opportunity for the student to discuss skill acquisition and enhancement. An established appointment, usually at least one hour per week, should be reserved.

Evaluation is twofold: it is an appraisal of the student's performance with suggestions for improvement, and it is an appraisal of the field placement program. The student should receive an honest appraisal of strengths and areas for improvement in a supportive manner at the midpoint and conclusion of the placement. Opportunities to improve areas of weakness should be provided. Problems which may not be readily resolved, or major infractions, should be reviewed with the department field placement coordinator. The program evaluation for the field placement ideally should include appraisals by the student(s), clients, supervisor(s), other staff members and the campus field placement coordinator, and it should discuss the program's strengths and weaknesses.

Professional Development. Many of the skills and nuances which culminate in a superior field placement take time to master and are learned by trial-and-error. The program staff can avoid pitfalls by engaging in preparatory activities. Such activities include reading books and journals about supervision, program administration, volunteerism, management and evaluation. Discussions led by those who have recently completed their field work are especially helpful. Other activities include attending field experience conferences and contacting local institutions and boards of education about continuing education programs. Examples of such programs and resource centers include the Certificate Program in Volunteer Management offered by Rutgers University (NJ) School of Social Work, The National VOLUNTEER Center (703-276-0542), the state or county Office of Volunteerism and the state Directors of Volunteers in Agencies (DOVIA).

CONCLUSION

A win-win situation is the desired outcome of field placements; it benefits the student, the agency and the campus. The student uses the placement to expand career options. The institution works in close conjunction with the student and field placement to ensure that the experience is credible, worthwhile and worthy of academic credit. And most importantly, those in need are helped.

SEXUAL ASSAULT AWARENESS PROGRAMMING

by K. C. Briskin & Juneau Mahan Gary

Educational presentations are one of the most effective strategies for promoting awareness and prevention of sexual assault. This chapter discusses the nuts and bolts of effective educational programs for students.

Campus sexual assault presentations require considerable preparation and planning because of the emotional content of the material. Many students exhibit denial, ignorance of the issues, and a reluctance to discuss the topics, usually because of the "it won't happen to me" syndrome. Effective presentations can occur in spite of audience resistance if attendance is required, such as in classes for athletic team meetings, and, by asking student groups, such as Greek organizations and residence floors, to require attendance. It is incumbent on the facilitators to make the presentation lively, engaging and informative for a captive audience so they will remain interested, and perhaps discuss their reactions with others.

PROGRAM CONTENT

Program content will vary depending upon the specific interests of the audience and the ability of the presenter. Several possible content areas for presentations follow.

Myths and Facts About Sexual Assault: It is helpful if facilitators ascertain the knowledge level of the audience and tailor the workshop accordingly. An informal "myths and facts" quiz, given at the beginning of the workshop, can be an excellent discussion generator among those unfamiliar with the topic. It can be answered by the group as a whole, or answered individually and then discussed in the group. (A sample quiz is found in *Appendix C.*) Discussion following the administration of the quiz will indicate areas of special interest or issues in need of clarification.

Date Rape: In general, the audience is interested in date rape because it is very prevalent on campuses. Ask the audience to respond to leading questions such as the following:

- What is "date rape?"

- What does date rape mean to you?

- Would you have to be on a date for this to occur?

- When is sex an appropriate part of a relationship?

- What do you think someone who is being pressured into sexual activity could do?

- What is the difference between consensual sex and coerced sex?

- How do you know when a person has consented to engaging in sex?

- Do women share any responsibility for the actions of a sexually aggressive man?

Following a general discussion of the questions, be prepared to present accurate information such as the following:

- The perception of date rape not being a legitimate sexual assault.

- How to recognize danger signs of date rape.

- Why date rape continues to happen.

- Why victims are reluctant to report it.

- What happens judicially if there is a charge of date rape.

- Knowing your limits and how to communicate them clearly.

Once date rape is understood, it is common for some audience members to redefine previous personal experiences as assaults. This insight enables them to understand that unwanted sexually aggressive behavior is a criminal act. Following the workshop, presenters should be available with referrals for participants who may need to work through some issues due to this realization.

Prevention of Sexual Assault: Most requests for presentations will be for prevention strategies to reduce the likelihood of a sexual assault. There are several excellent resources discussing prevention strategies. Burgess and Holmstrom (1979) provide a thorough list of safety precautions and a discussion of self-defense techniques. Hatcher, Atkinson, Cates, Glasser and Legins (1992) discuss the 1990's subject of "sexual etiquette" from a student-to-student perspective. The section "Ten Rules of Sexual Etiquette" (e.g., be sure sexual activity is consensual; "no" means "no") covers several prevention strategies for men and women for date rape and consenting sex situations. Pritchard (1988) and Kellen (1992) are other good resources. In addition, the municipal or campus police may be willing to supply and/or co-present this information.

Several issues should be covered in any discussion of sexual assault prevention and most chapters contain information for use in presentations. For instance, women can and should take basic precautions like locking doors or not walking alone in dangerous areas. In potential date rape situations, women need to be clear about their expectations and limits, and express them to their companions (as men do!). *Chapter 7* provides additional suggestions. Administrators should assess and strengthen campus security systems and should acquaint themselves with date rape and sexual assault issues. *Chapters 3, 4,* and *9* may be very helpful. Finally, a clear message must be sent to the campus community that sexual assault is not acceptable behavior. This is done through clear, well-publicized and enforced policies, comprehensive educational campaigns, and apprehension and appropriate discipline of offenders. By broadening the scope of discussion in this way, the tendency to blame the victim is minimized.

Resistance During an Attack: While exploring various methods of resistance, it is important for the presenters to stress that each situation is unique. Resistance may either scare off the offender or jeopardize the victim's safety; no one can predict if the offender will respond with violence or with retreat.

Audience members may want information about self-defense techniques during an attack. Discuss the advantages and disadvantages of the use of weapons and martial arts. Emphasize that a weapon can offer a feeling of control, but can also be forcibly taken during a struggle and used against her. Emphasize that the mastery of martial arts takes years of conscientious practice and a display of martial arts techniques is usually beyond the scope of one workshop. Refer interested students to the martial arts club or physical education department for technical instruction.

Close the presentation with a reminder that the important issue is for the victim to remain alive and that "resistance" can be psychological as well as physical. Considering the element of surprise, the probability of the attacker's greater size and strength and the possibility of a weapon, the victim needs to rely on her instincts and to be encouraged to do whatever she must to extricate herself from the situation and to prevent injury. Whatever she does to survive is the correct choice to make, even if she must submit. Submission does not mean consent and may, in fact, keep her alive.

Victim's Role Following an Assault: Frequently, the assault victim unwittingly destroys crucial evidence for prosecution because of her own ignorance, and this decreases alternatives for redress. This type of presentation highlights the importance of protecting physical evidence for the prosecution and the need to make informed decisions. This type of presentation is factual and didactic, covering the "do's" and "don'ts" following an assault. One way to get the audience to appreciate the role of the victim is to use an experiential exercise, such as a guided fantasy described later in this chapter. Following the exercise, ask the audience how they would respond. Many of the reactions, suggestions and procedures generated by the audience describe the initial impulse or natural reaction to cleanse the body after an assault. These reactions typically destroy physical evidence necessary for prosecution. Begin to classify the reactions, procedures and suggestions into a "do" list and a "don't" list, explaining why each was placed into the respective category.

The development and distribution of a list covering pertinent information is helpful. The handout allows for the audience to review the "do's" and "don'ts" at their own pace, as well as providing visual (i.e., handout) and auditory (i.e., workshop) learning. Please see *Appendix D* for a sample list. The list should cover the following facts:

- The victim should be discouraged from using any water; this includes bathing, douching, shampooing, drinking, brushing teeth and eating.

- The victim should be discouraged from changing clothes.

The victim should be discouraged from eliminating bodily wastes, if possible.

Choice Points: The assault survivor will have many decisions to make following an assault; these are called "choice points." She should be informed of her options and supported for her decisions so that she can begin to regain a sense of control over her life. It is important that she make her own choices (except in a severe medical emergency) as the ability to choose one's alternatives instills the feeling of regaining control. Some of the decisions must be made immediately while others can be postponed.

Some of the major "choice points" are whether to: (1) file a police report; (2) go to the hospital and receive emergency medical treatment; (3) prosecute; (4) inform her family and significant others; and (5) seek counseling. Encourage a discussion about the issues involved for each choice point while respecting one's value system. A summary of the choice points should be included in a handout.

Helping the Victim's Significant Others to Respond: The victim's significant others become secondary victims of the assault because of their relationship with the primary victim. As secondary victims, the general responses are usually feelings of helplessness, anger and rage. Sometimes these feelings are expressed by critical and judgmental remarks, rejection of the victim and the desire for revenge against the offender. Significant others can also respond with love, support and understanding. In most cases, they need guidance in knowing what to do and what not to do in order to help her to recover.

With this in mind, structuring a workshop with a list of "what to do" and "what not to do" for significant others is usually helpful. The "what not to do" list usually generates a discussion about feelings of helplessness, victimization, powerlessness and loss of control. Help the audience to recognize that examples of the "what not to do" list are not in their best interest to help the primary victim. Please see *Appendix E* for a sample list.

Ask the audience to generate a "what to do" list based on their perceptions of what a victim would need and from the perspective of helping her to regain control. Acknowledge that the significant others must confront two issues: supporting the victim and resolving their own personal reactions. Items might include the following:

- to demonstrate active listening skills;

- to let her make her own decisions;

- to take her reaction to the assault seriously;

- to be non-judgmental; and

- to let her know she is cared for.

Hilberman (1976), McEvoy and Brookings (1991), and Warshaw (1988) can be referred to for an extensive discussion on the reactions of significant others.

Special Populations: Special populations, such as lesbians, men, the disabled, racial minorities and virgins, often have needs which may not be obvious. For example, a victim with little or no previous sexual experience may react with greater intensity than other victims. She may question her desirability and self-worth as a woman more intensely than others, and may experience difficulty in differentiating between a sexual assault and consensual sex, having little basis for comparison. Some victims may experience a cultural or religious taboo regarding the assault. They may not know that they can seek help nor where to turn to for assistance. For detailed information on helping special populations, the reader is referred to Burgess and Holmstrom (1979), Friedman (1979), Russell (1982), Miller (1981), Zehner (1981) and Turetsky (1981).

Community Services: Be prepared to discuss local services for victims, including crisis intervention centers and victim support groups. Include referrals to the acute care hospital(s), police department, hotline program, counseling services and prosecutor's office. Provide telephone numbers, addresses and a contact person, if known, for each agency. Anticipate questions about how to start a crisis intervention program if none exists on campus. Carrow (1980), Adams and Abarbanel (1988), Parrot (1991), and Mills (1977) are excellent resources.

State Laws: Explain your state's laws on sexual assault and its enforcement. Include the strengths and weaknesses of the laws and their impact on the community, the victim and the offender. Review the campus judicial procedures for filing complaints and discuss the range of consequences the offender could receive from campus administrators. The presenter(s) should work in close collaboration with the campus police, municipal police, judicial officer and prosecutor's office in compiling legal information. NOW and Cherow-O'Leary (1987) describe women's legal rights about sexual assault and other related issues for each state. It reviews laws affecting women's lives and explains a woman's legal rights in a particular state. NOVA (Network of Victim Assistance) Chapters are located in many states and offer education/prevention programs and legal information.

What Can Students Do? This question tends to arise during a presentation. Assist the group to generate a list of concrete suggestions to reduce sexual assault, such as volunteer one's time and skills to a sexual assault organization, located either on or off campus. In addition to volunteer activities, presenters can suggest lobbying tactics or letter writing campaigns to campus and local newspapers. The problem of sexual violence is also an excellent topic for research papers in their social science and other classes. At the conclusion, distribute a list of what women, men and everyone can do to reduce sexual assault *(Appendix A)*. In this way, everyone can leave feeling empowered to reduce sexual assault and no one can leave with the perception that "there's nothing I can do to change things."

PRESENTATION TECHNIQUES

Because sexual assault is an emotionally charged topic, there is a need to consider several "how to's" which enhance a presentation. Described below are four general techniques to attend to when delivering presentations on sexual assault.

Atmosphere: Workshops are most effective when the material is organized and presented to gain maximum interest and attention. The tone and style of the presentation are important in "hooking" the attention of students. An open and honest group discussion, complemented by factual information, promotes a positive atmosphere.

Physical arrangements can contribute to or detract from an effective presentation. Optimal conditions necessitate relative privacy with minimal interruptions or distractions. Movable furniture can facilitate group interaction by its arrangement in a circle or semi-circle. A flexible furniture arrangement is also advantageous for experiential exercises and media presentations.

If addressing a large group, incorporate small group discussions as a part of the program. Of course, having a sufficient number of trained facilitators on hand is necessary.

Beginning and Ending a Presentation: Presenters should plan to arrive early in case some students wish to discuss their concerns beforehand about their expectations of the workshop or their personal experiences.

It is the responsibility of the presenters to put the audience at ease. Presenters should be prepared with group facilitation ideas to encourage participation and "break the ice." Presenters should identify themselves and their organization, make a brief self-disclosing introduction, and then have participants introduce themselves. The audience may be reluctant to discuss their feelings in front of others; therefore, give a brief introduction about sexual assault, use an experiential exercise, video or film to break the initial tension and encourage group participation. By this time, the program is usually well underway.

An empowering way to end the session is to encourage students to become active against sexual assault. List ways that individuals and groups can prevent sexual assault. Sponsor a contest (with a small award) between two or more groups to determine which group can generate the most comprehensive list. Before dismissing the group, ask participants to commit to accomplish at least one item on the list(s) generated in the session. See *Appendix A* for a list of projects. This technique leaves participants with positive feelings as they realize they can reduce sexual assault and it encourages individual responsibility. It is helpful to allow time for the possibility of referring a student who may be in crisis following the conclusion of the program.

Disseminating Material: Handouts with information or experiential exercises can be very helpful, especially for the student who is not an auditory learner. Handouts allow students to process visual material at their own rate and at their individual level of comfort. Written material also provides a mechanism for students to share the information with others who were not present, thereby increasing the impact of the presentation.

Handouts could include a campus newsletter (see *Appendix F)* and program brochures. Promotional giveaways are useful when they contain important and emergency campus extensions and have some practical application (e.g., key chain, magnets, pencils).

Most organizations willingly share written material and encourage its dissemination, so it is not necessary to "re-invent the wheel" by re-creating the same material; simply acknowledge the original source. Also, include the organization's name, address and telephone number on the material to facilitate future contact.

Experiential Exercises: Experiential exercises are useful tools to incorporate into a presentation. This section contains several examples, The timely interjection of an exercise can break the monotony of the lecture, which may too closely resemble a college course. These exercises can be less threatening and more succinct and effective vehicles for learning compared to traditional college classroom experiences Most students have an intellectual awareness of sexual assault and experiential exercises can produce the visceral, or "gut," realization of its impact. The exercises provide a great potential for education by one's peers through group interaction, and they encourage participants to examine their personal beliefs and attitudes. The process of self-examination and self-awareness tends to increase the personal relevance of the material presented.

As a precaution, be cognizant that not all members of the audience will feel comfortable participating in experiential exercises. Participation in the exercises may evoke strong emotional reactions or uncomfortable and negative memories of past experiences. Assure the audience that participation is voluntary; those choosing not to participate are still encouraged to contribute to the discussion. If possible, arrange to have someone available for further discussion or referral following the program.

Examples of experiential exercises are outlined below.

Example A: Myths and Facts Quiz (see *Appendix C)*

Myths about sexual assault are prevalent. A quiz is helpful when administered at the beginning of a workshop because it enables presenters to ascertain the group's knowledge level, to gear the workshop accordingly and to facilitate group discussion. A "rape questionnaire," similar to the quiz, is described by McCombie (1980) and can be used also.

Example B: Guided Fantasy

The guided fantasy exercise assists the audience to safely place themselves into a fantasy of violence and assault, and to experience some of the feelings. Emphasize that participation is voluntary. Read the script in a slow and calm manner. The audience is instructed to:

"Sit or lie back, close your eyes and make yourself comfortable. I want you to relax and try to drain your mind of distracting thoughts and put yourself in the scene which I am about to describe."

You're on a date with the friend of a friend. He's a nice guy and he makes you laugh. The movie you saw was good, although the way he touched your knee and hair was a little too friendly. But you ignored it because you didn't want to make a scene. Now after the movie, it's still early and he suggests a walk by the lake. You walk together for a long while and you begin to feel uneasy. He turns to kiss you and then starts to unbutton your blouse. You tell him 'no,' that you don't feel comfortable, but he ignores you and continues. You try to stop him and he slaps you. You struggle and he knocks you to the ground.

Following the fantasy, ask the audience to remain in the scene and to experience their emotions for about thirty seconds. Afterwards, encourage them to discuss their emotions and reactions. Prepare discussion questions in case participants are reluctant to respond voluntarily. Ask the following:

- What reactions and emotions were you most aware of?

- If you were the man, what would you do differently and when would you do it? Why then?

- If you were the woman, what would you do differently and when would you do it? Why then?

- How would you help the woman understand what happened?

- How would you help the man understand what happened?

The guided fantasy portrayed the early stages of a date rape. When it is used with an audience of women, most will usually be able to identify with the victim. This scenario follows the four-step pattern of date rape as outlined by Parrot and Link (1983). Briefly, the steps are: (1) violating a woman's personal space, (2) perceiving no visible discomfort or resistance by the victim, (3) ending up in a secluded place, and (4) raping the victim. This scenario can be used to explain the pattern of date rapes, to explore the audience's perceptions of victim and offender responsibility, and to brainstorm possible prevention strategies, including assertive communication and intervention at the first sign of discomfort.

A guided fantasy must be used with caution because of the possibility of anonymous assault victims in the audience identifying too closely with the scenario. It is essential to process the audience's reactions and feelings to the exercise. It is likely that a participant may want to stay after the program has concluded to share a similar incident. Allow time for this possibility and provide appropriate referrals.

Example C: Role Plays

Role plays "set the stage" for participants to experience an assault or attempted assault from a safe distance, as is the case with the guided fantasy exercise. They help participants (a) to identify with a victim's fear and to experience some of the uncertainties in a given situation; and (b) to feel some of the emotions that a significant other might experience. Role plays work best with a sophisticated and mature audience who can handle the anxiety.

Role Play #1:   You return from a first date. Your hair is disheveled and your clothes are torn slightly. A friend asks "what happened?"

Role Play #2:   You've just been sexually assaulted near your car on campus. You notice a passerby approaching in your direction.

As with the guided fantasy, role plays should be used with caution. The debriefing process following the role play is important for the players and audience because it gets role players "out of character" and into their real experiences. Moreover, it brings the audience and role players back to the present and gives everyone the opportunity and outlet to discuss reactions and alternative responses.

Example D: Attitudes Toward Sexual Assault Scale

Parrot (1988) uses a Likert-type continuum scale with the purpose of helping participants to evaluate their personal values and attitudes toward sexual assault. Participants are asked to indicate their level of agreement to a set of statements of extreme positions about sexual assault based on a one-to-five scale such as "society condones rape" . . . "society condemns rape." Following completion of the scale, participants share and discuss their responses.

Example E: Panel Presentation

This can be an excellent model for a program offered to students. The issues can be discussed in a panel presentation composed of students, administrators and, if possible, a student who was a sexual assault victim and willing to share the experience. The panel allows an examination of the issues from different perspectives. The added participation of a victim can have a great impact on the audience. With self-disclosure by a peer, sexual assault ceases to be theoretical and becomes reality in that it can happen to any student. This can be a powerfully insightful moment.

RECOMMENDATIONS

Thus far, this chapter has focused on the nuts and bolts of effective sexual assault programs. This section offers recommendations for effective implementation of sexual assault programs on campus. Several issues beyond date, time and place must be addressed to ensure a successful program. These issues include the following: cooperation with campus and community organizations; background information about the sponsoring organization or group; audience composition; negotiation of responsibilities; publicity; physical arrangements; and evaluation. Each topic is addressed below.

Sponsoring Groups: Presentations which are arranged through existing or sponsoring groups (e.g., Psychology Club, Greek Letter organizations, a course, a residence floor) usually have good attendance because they have a built-in membership or can require attendance. Compile relevant information about the group needs. Ask the following types of questions: What are the reasons for the workshop request? Has there been a recent assault?   What are the needs of the sponsoring organization?   What does the organization wish to accomplish as a result of the workshop?   Responses to these types of questions can assist the presenter(s) to tailor the workshop to the needs of the sponsoring organization's audience.

Audience Composition: Inquire about the size and composition of the anticipated audience. What will be the audience's age range, gender, race and level of familiarity with the subject? Will there be identified victims present, and will they be sharing their experiences? Will the audience attend on a voluntary or mandatory basis? Is the audience expected to be receptive or resistant to the topic?

A class is an involuntary group because attendance is required; therefore, for this type of workshop, presenter(s) should select a topic and organize the material to gain immediate and maximum interest and attention. Presentations in which students attend voluntarily contain a self-selected audience with a greater interest level and less resistance. This latter group allows the presenter greater freedom in methods of presentation.   Both men and women benefit from such educational programming.

Logistics: Develop a clear understanding of each party's responsibilities and contributions toward a successful presentation. A checklist should be devised to establish agreement for the completion of tasks.   The checklist can include items such as: publicity, logistical arrangements, equipment rentals and set up, reproduction of printed material and room reservation.

Publicity: Ask the sponsoring organization to be responsible for publicity development and dissemination.   Offer to preview the advertisements. Act as a consultant by giving constructive feedback and suggestions to avoid the distribution of inaccurate or misleading information. Suggest innovative locations and specific resources to publicize the event. Word-of-mouth promotion by the sponsoring organization usually proves to be the most effective advertisement.

Male attendance is crucial as most men still perceive sexual assault as a woman's issue. They seldom realize the role men have in causing and reducing sexual assault. Target predominantly male groups such as fraternities, Engineering Club and athletes. Encourage the advisor, president, chairperson or coach to require attendance.

Evaluation: Evaluation of the presentation can help to improve and refine future workshops. At least three kinds of information are helpful: an evaluation form, informal feedback and peer critique.

A short *evaluation form* provides immediate and direct reactions to the presentation. Through this method, reactions can be gathered from a diversity of individuals. *Informal feedback* can be obtained by contacting a member of the sponsoring organization several weeks following the workshop. Inquire about the presentation style, delivery and observations of lasting impact, such as behavioral changes. Finally, verbal and written *critique from an informed peer* who attended the workshop can offer insight. The critique should include a technical and general evaluation from someone familiar with sexual assault concerns.

DATE RAPE AWARENESS PROGRAMMING

by M. Aizenman, C. Andrews, P.H. Witt & W.D. Burns

Large numbers of college students are faced with situations which can lead to date rape. Some students tend to believe naively that they are immune to sexual assault and date rape because, for example, they attend a small private college rather than a large inner-city university. Nothing could be further from the truth. Sexual assault is not limited to urban universities; it takes place on all kinds of campuses.

With this in mind, perhaps the most important population in need of sensitization about sexual assault is students. Women must be made aware of the risks and dangers existing on the campus and must learn strategies to avoid an assault. Likewise, men are also in need of awareness and prevention programs which reduce offensive and illegal behavior. Men can be supportive of and sensitive to the women in their lives and learn to understand the subtleties between consensual sex and sexual assault.

New students, fraternity and sorority members, resident students and male athletes should be targeted for educational programming. First year students especially should be educated because a large number of date rapes occur during the first two years of college. If possible, new student orientation should devote considerable attention to the risks, realities and prevention of date rape with special attention focused on the role of alcohol consumption contributing to date rape. Moreover, many persons and groups such as fraternity and sorority members and athletes tend to support and promote the sex role stereotyping that is at the root of the problem. Clearly, they too need special programs to promote rape awareness.

CHAPTER 7

AWARENESS PROGRAMS

Effective awareness and education about sexual assault require a focus on the definition, incidence, prevalence and strategies to reduce risk. They require the cultivation of one's sense of obligation arising from membership in a community, accompanied with care and concern about human dignity, in addition to effective communication and "refusal" skills. Equally important, though, it is necessary to go beyond the "rights and rules" approach to prevention and education, to the special problems of the "self in relation to others." Theories of the self that overemphasize individualism and autonomy in all things may obscure subtle coercion and exaggerate the tendency to see any consequence that befalls a person as being self-generated. Such views often encourage "blaming the victim." From the vantage point of hindsight, the prevention programs based on such theories paralyze women's lives as long as men are free to try to "get what they want" and women are forced to devise protection and avoidance strategies to combat sexual assault.

Most awareness programs can be presented by the student life staff or peer educators who are trained in group facilitation skills. Peer educators are usually preferable to student life staff because they can transcend the student-authority figure barrier. They relate student-to-student and can confront their peers because they intimately understand and are part of the student culture.

Ideally, programs should be incorporated into required courses such as "Freshman Seminar," with messages about sexual assault and date rape reinforced in other communications with students (e.g., articles in the student newspaper, newsletters, peer education programs). Programs should include the role of other societal and cultural influences which contribute to sexual assault and which influence students' attitudes, values and development. In essence, date rape cannot be addressed separately from the topics of sexuality, sex roles, communication skills, assertiveness, self-esteem or substance abuse.

Date Rape. The following facts should be emphasized when date rape is discussed by those responsible for awareness or prevention programming.

- It may not be recognized as "real rape" by the victim, the victim's friends or relatives or by the public. This results from the erroneous perception that "real rapes" are perpetrated by strangers, not by someone known to the victim (Bridges, 1991). Date rapes *are* rapes and must be treated as such.

- It tends to take place on second or third dates, since many women are more cautious on first dates or at initial meetings.

- It tends to happen in situations where the offender and victim are not emotionally involved, usually after an initial meeting or between two friends in a residence hall.

- It usually takes place in the residence of the offender or victim. Loud music is often playing before and during the rape to muffle sounds and screams.

- It frequently results from aggressive male behavior combined with one or more of the following:

  a) A lack of clear understanding about the intention(s) and expectation(s) of both people;

  b) A lack of assertive behavior by the victim;

  c) Victim vulnerability resulting from substance abuse, stress, fatigue or personality (e.g., low self-esteem); and

  d) Aggression by the offender which is exacerbated by substance abuse, peer pressure, or his inability to distinguish aggression from "masculinity."

- Victims of date rape frequently tend to feel more ashamed, guilty and depressed than victims of stranger rape. Their guilt stems from the initial choice to be in the company of the offender. Furthermore, because they knew the person and perhaps made a value judgment that the person was trustworthy, they tend to assume that *they* must be at fault. Of course, this feeling of blame on the part of victims is entirely erroneous. Victims are *never* responsible for being raped. They often lose confidence in their ability to judge and trust others; they believe they can no longer tell the "good guys" from the "bad guys." This can make subsequent socialization very difficult.

- Since many victims feel guilty, many are unlikely to discuss the incident or report it. Consequently, these victims seldom seek medical treatment or counseling and may drop out of college.

- Alcohol and substance abuse can increase the frequency and intensity of aggressive behavior by altering internal controls of the offender and victim.

Armed with the above facts, read the following two case studies. See how many facts are evident in these typical campus date rape situations. Note the divergent perspectives of the man and woman.

Case No. 1: "Bob and Patty: A Study Gone Awry"

Bob: *Patty and I were in the same statistics class together. She usually sat near me and was always very friendly. I liked her and thought maybe she liked me too. Last Thursday I decided to find out. After class I suggested that she come to my place to study for midterms together. She agreed immediately, which was a good sign. That night everything seemed to go perfectly. We studied for a while and then took a break. I could tell that she really liked me, and I was attracted to her. I was getting excited. I started kissing her. I could tell that she really liked it. We started touching each other, and it felt really good. All of a sudden she pulled away and said "Stop." I figured she didn't want me to think that she was easy or loose. A lot of women think they have to say 'no' at first. I knew once I showed her what a good time she could have, and that I would respect her in the morning, it would be okay. I just ignored her protests and eventually she stopped struggling. I think she liked it but afterwards she acted bummed out and cold. Who knows what the problem was?"*

Patty: *I knew Bob from my statistics class. He's cute and we are both good at statistics, so when a tough midterm was scheduled, I was glad that he suggested we study together. It never occurred to me that it was anything except a study date. That night everything went fine at first, we got a lot of studying done in a short amount of time so when he suggested we take a break, I thought we deserved it. Well, all of a sudden he started acting really romantic and started kissing me. I liked the kissing but then he started touching me below the waist. I pulled away and tried to stop him but he didn't listen. After a while I stopped struggling; he was so much bigger and stronger than me. I couldn't believe it was happening to me. I didn't know what to do. He actually forced me to have* *sex with him. I guess, looking back on it, I should have screamed or done something besides trying to reason with him, but it was so unexpected. I couldn't believe it was happening. I still can't believe it did."*

Case No. 2: "Phil and Cindy: The Same Story But Two Different Points of View"

Phil: *"I still don't understand what happened. Cindy and I had been dating for about two months and while we had not slept together yet, I had certainly made it clear that I was attracted to her and eventually expected to have sex with her. We were supposed to go to a party, and when she showed up in this sexy low-cut dress, I thought maybe this was her way of saying she was ready. At the party we drank some beer, which made her sort of sleepy and sensual. When she said she wanted to go lie down and have me come snuggle with her, what was I supposed to think? Of course I thought she wanted to have sex. Granted, she did grumble a little when I started to undress her, but I just figured she wanted to be persuaded. Lots of women feel a little funny about being forward, and want men to take responsibility for sex. I don't know. We had sex, and it was fine. I took her home from the party, and thought everything was okay. But ever since then she refuses to talk to me or go out with me. I thought she really liked me. What happened?"*

Cindy: *"I'll never forget that night as long as I live. Phil and I had been dating a while, and he had always acted like a perfect gentleman. Well, we had done our share of kissing, but he never gave me any reason not to trust him. The night of the party I wore this gorgeous dress that I borrowed from my roommate. It was a little flashier than I normally wear, but I thought it was very flattering. At the party I had some beer, and it really made me tired so I wanted to lie down. Maybe I shouldn't have suggested that we both lie down together, but it felt weird to just go upstairs by myself and leave Phil all alone. The next thing I knew he was all over me, forcing me to have sex with him. It was horrible. I didn't want to scream and make a fool of myself with all those other people in the next room, but I tried to fight him off. I guess I was just too wiped out to be very effective. Needless to say, I never want to see Phil again. He seemed like such a nice guy. What happened?" (Hughes, O'Gorman & Sandler, 1987).*

Clearly, in both case studies, there was a lack of communication about the expectations of the date. The men did not see their aggressive behavior as "rape" and actually thought the women enjoyed it. Conversely, the women felt sexually abused and betrayed by the act of violence exhibited by the men.

Coercive Sex. Legally, rape is defined in two terms: (a) by the rapist using force or threat of force, and (b) by the victim acting against her will. However, there are other types of coercion to which victims may be subjected such as the man promising, threatening, manipulating or lying in order to coerce the woman into doing something against her will. Neither overt violence nor the threat of violence is involved. This type of coercion is frequent in relationships and is exemplified in the following four situations: (1) he tells her that he will marry her if she will make love with him (or will not marry her if she does not); (2) he and his peers tell her that it is unnatural not to have sex or to be a virgin; (3) he threatens to terminate the relationship if she will not have sex with him (or participate in some act that she finds undesirable); and (4) after a degree of intimacy he proclaims "sexual rights" over her. Although there is nothing illegal about such manipulative communications, these subtle forms of coercion should be the basis for discussion about healthy and unhealthy dating relationships.

In a coercive situation, it is very important for women to communicate their feelings accurately, assertively and at the first sign of intimidation. For example, women should not let men patronize them, especially when feelings and values are concerned. They should communicate clearly that they do not want to engage in certain behaviors. In order to avoid miscommunication, women should be encouraged to consider carefully what sexual interaction, if any, they want to have with a partner. If they know what they want, they will be less likely to send messages that may be misinterpreted. Women should be encouraged to present consistency between their verbal and nonverbal messages, and they should be cognizant of "male perspectives" of dating as well. To help understand the "male perspective" of dating, Parrot and Link (1983) investigated reasons given by men when attempting to have sexual relations with a woman against her will. Eight erroneous reasons are mentioned below:

1. The woman asked the man for the date and appeared to be pursuing him;

2. The couple went to an apartment or secluded place rather than to a public place;

3. The man paid for all of the expenses;

4. They dated for a long time;

5. The woman said she would have sex and changed her mind;

6. The woman touched the man's penis or engaged in other foreplay;

7. The woman let the man touch her breasts or legs; and

8. The woman got drunk or high.

Ask women the following question, "When you feel uncomfortable about his advances, do you acquiesce or do you say 'no'?" The next time it occurs, consider the following before you decide:

- The man may be lying. A promise to marry based on your agreement to have sexual relations can be broken easily and short-lived.

- In lasting, healthy relationships, both parties must learn to negotiate.

- This process begins while dating. A healthy relationship builds trust which is the foundation of good, solid friendships.

- Saying "no" when you mean "no" can result in your boyfriend and peers respecting you more than if you must "go along." On the other hand, if your boyfriend decided to move on to "greener pastures," will his leaving be a real loss? The same question, of course, applies to "friends."

- Your real friends will not exert peer pressure to coerce you into doing something you really don't want to do.

One way to reduce sexual coercion is if women learn to honestly communicate their feelings to dating partners. When a woman says "no" and means it, it is incumbent upon her to be very clear about her feelings. Use the following examples for clarification: you can say "please don't" in a shy, soft voice (which the male may construe as "yes" or as token resistance); you can say "no" in a loud voice; or you can scream "Get your hands off of my body." Most women can hear, see and feel the heightened intensity in the three requests and are in a position to make the appropriate response based on the specific situation. If he continues to ignore her feelings or displays behavior which she finds offensive, she should be assertive and not concern herself about whether he or others may think she is rude. If he accuses her of being suspicious of his intentions, she should communicate that she has a right to be cautious. If his feelings get hurt, she should not feel guilty. Her goal is to protect herself.

Awareness Programs for Men. Unfortunately, the problem of sexual assault and date rape have been perceived as primarily a woman's problem. Scant attention has been given to the role that men play in perpetuating sexual assault, or to their role in assisting women to recover from the trauma. Statistics indicate that women represent about 98 percent of victims and men almost exclusively are the offenders. During the last decade, studies have pieced together a picture of what causes men to coerce women into sexual activity. Groth (1979) notes that rape is the sexual expression of aggression and rapists rape for power. If one examines the more frequent campus occurrence of a man coercing a woman into sexual activity, what seems to emerge is that men are not identifying some of their behavior as being sexually aggressive and are unaware of what constitutes rape and sexually aggressive behavior.

Typically, offenders have little comprehension of the potential negative consequences of their coercive sexual acts. They cite several reasons for the lack of awareness, including (a) their perception that the aberrant behavior was acceptable; (b) their presumption that the victim enjoyed the sexual attention; and (c) their perception of a lack of apparent consequences because their behavior was seldom or never reported to the judicial officer or campus police. Many *convicted* sex offenders have stated that they repeatedly performed their sexually offensive behavior without apprehension and assumed there would be no consequence!

Awareness training for men is necessary so that men can re-evaluate their behaviors and attitudes about women, sex and sexuality (Baier, Rosenzweig & Whipple, 1991; Bridges, 1991). To adequately confront the problem of sexual assault on campus, there must be an understanding by men and women that the problem exists. With acknowledgment of the problem, prevention and awareness programs can be effective. Some effective programs will be discussed below.

Most prevention and awareness programs have focused on the victims (women) rather than on the offenders (men) in attempting to prevent sexual assaults. The traditional, yet limited approach, would seem to account for only a portion of the solution and would seem to implicitly blame the victim. A non-traditional and broad approach would seem to have greater efficacy in promoting awareness in comparison to the traditional model. Egidio and Robertson (1981), Lee (1987) and Willmarth (1985) have designed non-traditional programs targeted exclusively for men. They developed awareness and experiential programs which attempt to prevent sexual assaults by men and to increase male self-awareness. The programs review myths and facts, examine attitudes and behaviors, and discuss types of personal and political actions men can take to help prevent sexual assault. Generally, they used male group leaders or peer educators based on the assumption that men will talk more openly in an all-male setting than they would in a male-female setting.

Another type of male awareness program focuses on values clarification. Men can be helped to understand how society instills values, attitudes and behaviors in individuals while they re-evaluate their current attitudes and behaviors toward women and sex. Beneke (1983) can be used as a resource to develop a male-oriented values clarification workshop.

Another topic is discussing "Rape Language" in which men tend to structure their experiences about women through metaphors (Beneke, 1983). That is, having sex is an achievement; the achievement is gaining possession of a valued commodity; and the valued commodity is a woman's body. The woman who is a commodity tends to be perceived as an "object" rather than as a human being, and this may partially account for the low rate of acknowledgment of sexually aggressive behavior among men. Examples of rape language include the following:

a) **Sex is achievement**: I didn't work very hard to get into her pants.

b) **Sex is a hunt or conquest**: I'm going to get a piece of a-- tonight.

c) **Sex is a game**: I hope I score tonight.

d) **Sex is war**: He's always hunting women.

e) **Sex is being serviced by a woman**: She did it for him but wouldn't do it for me.

f) **Sex is instruction**: You could learn a lot from me, baby.

g) **Sex is a commodity**: I've never had to pay for pussy.

h) **Sex is possession**: I'd like to have her for the night.

i) **Sex is convenient**: She's easy.

A fourth type of workshop, loosely called "Blaming the Victim (or She Asked for It)" is a different approach to helping men understand their attitudes and behaviors toward women. Men can be encouraged to discuss the following situations which contain myths and misconceptions about date rape:

a) If a woman trusts a man and goes on a date or returns to his room and is sexually assaulted, then she is a dupe. He did not really rape her, he just took advantage of her.

b) If a woman is seen as attractive by men and dresses for attractiveness, then she attacked him with her weapon; he must counter-attack with his weapon.

c) When a woman says "no," it means "yes" to a man. Men are confused and incredulous when a woman is raped, especially in a dating situation, because in their experience, women cannot be believed. Clearly, the issue of "implied consent" is a critical topic to discuss in workshops with male students.

Men can be helped to search for a genuine and masculine identity which debunks the often-held belief that the sexual act is the necessary proof of masculinity. Moreover, educational programs should stress that some men also feel abused in dating relationships, and report that they have been coerced to engage in sexual relations against their will. This information may reduce some male defensiveness and denial. Many times when these programs occur, men feel attacked and resentful for being placed in the role of the offender. These feelings increase tension, reduce their ability to be receptive to the woman's perspective and decrease their motivation to change behavior.

Group or Party Rape. In a group rape, several men take turns raping a woman. They are also called party and gang rapes. Male students usually follow the lead of an older student's peer pressure without regard for the welfare of the victim(s). The following statement provides an understanding of the extent of the problem of gang rape:

> *When the Project on the Status and Education of Women first heard of incidents (of gang rapes on campuses), we initially believed that they were isolated occurrences. However, as we gathered more information we began to realize that these events were not single aberrations but events that happen all too commonly on too many campuses. (We) identified more that 50 incidents occurring at a wide range of institutions: public, private, religiously affiliated, Ivy League, large and small. On some campuses, Project staff were told 'it happens almost every week.' Apparently, no institution is immune from the potential of 'fraternity gang rape' or 'party gang rape' (Ehrhart & Sandler, 1985).*

The fact that such gang rapes are prevalent, and especially associated with fraternities and athletes, places a heavy and unfair burden on women to remain alert. If a woman gets drunk or high, some men will view her as an easy target for a gang rape because she is perceived as vulnerable. By contrast, if a man gets drunk or high, it is unlikely that anyone will make sexual advances toward him. The following is a typical campus scenario:

> *The 17 year old freshman went to a fraternity's "little sister" party with two of her roommates and they left early without her. She was trying to get a ride home when a fraternity brother told her he would take her after the party ended. While she waited, two other fraternity members took her to a bedroom to "discuss little sister matters." The door was closed and one of the brothers stood blocking the exit.*

> *They told her that in order to become a little sister (an honorary member) she would have to have sex with a fraternity member. She was frightened, fearing they would physically harm her if she refused. She could see no escape. Each of the brothers had sex with her, as did a third who had been hiding in the room.*

> *During the next two hours, a succession of men went into the room. There were never fewer than three men with her, sometimes more. After they let her go, a fraternity brother drove her home. He told her not to feel bad about the incident because*

another woman had also been 'upstairs' earlier that night (Ehrhart & Sandler, 1985).

Accurate and accessible information can help to reduce or prevent the incidence of group rape. Consult Pritchard (1988) for further information and review the following facts about group rape:

- Most gang rapes are associated with fraternities and athletic teams, although they do not all take place in fraternity house settings; some occur in residence halls and at off-campus parties.

- Voyeurism is often associated with gang rapes; those not directly involved in the assault may watch others and are culpable as well.

- Substance abuse is almost always associated with campus gang rapes.

- Fraternity gang rapes are often planned in advance; it is just a matter of finding a victim.

CONCLUSION

Date rape awareness programming is a constant requirement on campus because of students' feelings of invincibility, denial of sexual assault personally affecting their lives and constant student turnover. Peer educators can educate other students effectively and with far reaching results in comparison to the student life staff. Programs should clearly focus on women *and* men to decrease campus assaults and to educate about what constitutes date rape and sexual assault.

TRAINING FOR CAMPUS ADMINISTRATORS

by M. Aizenman & G. Kelley

College administrators are often not aware of the frequency or effects of sexual assaults and date rapes on their campuses. This is due, in part, to stereotypes about where and how often sexual assault occurs on campus and to the reluctance of students to report date rape. Researchers have revealed that the incidence and prevalence of sexual assault, and especially date rape, are significantly higher than one would expect (Baier, Rosenweig & Whipple, 1991). Further, the research indicates that students are unclear as to what constitutes appropriate and inappropriate sexual behavior

It is of primary importance for administrators to appoint a committee composed of a cross-section of the campus community to develop a policy delineating acceptable sexual conduct, clarifying penalties for digressions, and publicizing the policy. Usually a "sexual conduct" policy can be built upon a school's existing conduct policy. While a policy on acceptable sexual behavior might be merged with a sexual harassment policy, for example, separate guidelines are preferable as the distinction will most likely emphasize the significance of each problem. Similarly, procedures for assisting a victim should be described clearly and be made visible to the students as well as to faculty and administrators who might be the victim's first contact following the assault. Administrators also need to be active in developing effective judicial procedures and services which appropriately assist victims. A procedure to disseminate factual and non-confidential information to the campus and surrounding community should be established. Procedures such as these will ensure compliance with the Campus Awareness and Securtiy Act. Finally, how and who will handle off-campus communications with parties, such as the victim's relatives, friends, reporters, hospital personnel and municipal police needs to be clarified.

TRAINING FOR ADMINISTRATORS AND STAFF

There are several approaches to implementing effective in-service training programs on date rape for campus administrators and staff. When developing effective programs, it is important to gain support and legitimacy by establishing a planning committee representing a cross-section of informed and concerned staff, faculty, students and community residents. Such a committee might consist of the following administration representatives: director of campus Sexual Assault Program (chair), Residence Director, Department of Women's Studies, Campus Police, Counseling, Health Center, General Counsel, Dean of Students, Substance Abuse Education or Health Education, Minority Affairs, students and community representatives. Student representation might include the following: one undergraduate, one graduate student, one peer educator, one fraternity/sorority member, one athlete and one student government or residence housing member. At least one of these students should be a resident student, a person of color, a male and a commuting student. Community representatives might include the following: municipal police, mayor or county executive, sexual assault program, hospital and counseling agency.

The committee should consider a two-step training format. The initial session covers general information about rape which is of interest to a cross-section of campus participants. The second step consists of follow-up sessions with individual offices to discuss technical and specific issues related to the specialty of the office staff. The planning committee should not "reinvent the wheel" in designing a program, but should utilize existing campus and local resources as a way of strengthening the institution's relationship with staff, faculty, and community agencies. An administration will frequently seek highly visible national and international experts, and overlook local and campus authorities. One major advantage of the local expert is familiarity with the problem, possession of accurate statistics, knowledge of accepted campus mores and familiarity with available resources. It would be preferable to use this opportunity to develop or strengthen relationships with local and campus experts who will work consistently to be effective with interventions, instead of an "expert" who will make one visit to campus. This is not to imply that national and international experts do not serve an important purpose; they do. They should be one piece of several pieces which constitute a truly effective prevention and intervention program.

Occupational Groups. Follow-up programs (i.e., step two) for each office unit should be conducted to focus on specific issues of occupational relevance, and several are discussed below. This will enable each occupational unit to understand and prepare for their role in assisting victims. The following is a review of which offices should be included in campus-wide training and what specific topics should be covered:

Police or Security Department. When the offender is known to the victim, legal questions and issues can be extremely complex and confusing. Date rapes are usually not reported directly to the police. However, when a student reports the rape, most campus police and security units are amenable to holding an informal discussion with the victim. The purpose is to explain legal procedures and reporting policies without necessarily filing any formal charges. Police officers may have received training at the police academy in handling sexual assaults and in basic crisis intervention techniques. On the other hand, security officers may have little or no previous training in comparison to police officers. On campuses where security officers are employed instead of police officers, the administration should maintain a strong and positive relationship with the municipal police.

Health Center Staff. A nurse or physician is likely to "accidently" encounter a student who was involved in a rape, perhaps months or years after the incident. The "accidental" discovery may result from the student answering routine medical questions unrelated to the student's current reasons for seeking medical treatment. Even if a student seeks medical assistance for a pelvic examination following a rape without reporting it as such, the staff can place the student at ease and ask appropriate questions after attending to the student's present problem. Examinations for sexual assault are delicate and complicated procedures. The student, if willing, should be referred to the hospital designated for sexual assault examinations. One training topic for Health Center staff can focus on the effective and timely referral of a student for the sexual assault examination. Finally, students tend to seek help too late for the collection of physical evidence. The staff should be refreshed in making effective referrals on campus, such as to the police or counseling center.

Residence Hall Staff. This is the group who will often be the initial contact for students reporting an assault. Date rapes are usually revealed to friends of the victim, who, in turn, report the assault to residence staff. The issues of handling indirect reporting situations, as well as establishing a procedure to handle these cases in general, should be addressed. Recommendations for an effective residence life procedure include a review of informal enforcement procedures; sponsoring educational programs; directing the judicial officer to implement informal or formal judicial proceedings against male students who have been charged with rape. The unofficial and informal methods can be used when the victim does not want to pursue formal judicial procedures which are usually significantly traumatic.

Judicial Officer. If a rape is brought to the judicial level, both parties must be interviewed in an objective manner so as to not place premature guilt on either party. The judicial officer, in consultation with the victim, will decide if the offender should be charged and if so, if the proceedings will be informal or formal.

The judicial staff should be briefed on the psychological trauma which the victim may experience and must understand and appreciate that the victim may not be able to remember the details of the rape because of the physical and emotional trauma. The victim may repress the incident and may be unable to recall a clear picture of the details. In fact, during different interviews, she may recall slight alterations of detail resulting from the impact of repression, denial or other reactions to the trauma.

Academic Advisors. Academic performance can be significantly effected by the trauma following a rape. Trauma can result in poor concentration, missed examinations and poor grades. The student may confide in the academic advisor about a sexual assault, depending on the nature of their relationship. Or, an astute advisor may inquire about the student's drastic change in academic behavior and be informed about the assault. It should be emphasized though, that only a victim can disclose this information, or, if the victim consents, that someone else (e.g., counselor, nurse) can communicate for her.

Training for advisors may include active listening skills, basic crisis intervention techniques and effective referral strategies. This repertoire will enable the advisor to be sensitive to the immediate and long term needs of the student in crisis. The advisor should assist the victim in resuming academic studies within a safe, sensitive and supportive environment and may intervene in approaching professors about extending deadlines by explaining the student's situation using general terms (e.g., personal problems, medical emergency), without revealing specific details.

Counselors. Counselors report that victims of rape underutilize counseling services. However, the significant psychological and emotional trauma and accompanying clinical issues suggest the need for counseling. A competent counselor without specific expertise in sexual assault issues can usually have limited efficacy. However, specific skills can increase the counselor's repertoire and ability to counsel victims effectively. One or two training sessions should review the major features of rape crisis trauma and post-traumatic stress syndrome. A local sexual assault counselor could facilitate the session and incorporate case studies, role plays and experiential exercises.

Counselors should develop skills for assessing offenders as well. Assessment sessions should focus clearly on the clinical issues. One common failure of otherwise competent counselors who do not have this specific expertise is a lack of focus on the deviant sexual behavior and thought processes. If not addressed directly, counseling could well result in a student who still experiences deviant sexual urges, thus continuing to place him and potential victims at risk for further offenses. The counselor should locate clinicians in the geographic area who have expertise with sexual assault offenders. They should seek referrals from colleagues, the state psychological association or a county psychological association. Moreover, not every counselor can work or chooses to work with offenders.

Clergy. The clergy are often overlooked for sexual assault awareness training on campus. Yet, depending on the student's spiritual background, a cleric may be the only person on campus in which the student (i.e., victim or offender) confides. The self-disclosure could be twofold: to seek emotional support and to seek spiritual guidance. For the victim, she may experience confusion about her role in the assault and the limits of her responsibility. For the offender, he may seek spiritual guidance and support (although this does not happen frequently) and request the cleric to accompany him to the police station or judicial hearing.

Campus clergy should be trained in basic crisis intervention techniques and active listening skills. Further, a two-way communication network should be established to help clergy to be cognizant of how and when to make referrals on campus as well as for campus staff to be cognizant of how and when to make referrals to clergy regarding rape.

First Responder. All staff and administrators who may be the first to respond to the victim should be trained in responding effectively to her needs. Individuals such as the following should be involved: campus police/security (including student staff), health center staff, counselors, residence life staff (including student staff) and sexual assault support persons. The session should stress that one's attitude, manner and competence can be more important than one's gender. The "do's" and "don'ts" for effective victim assistance should be reviewed. Briefly, the "do's" include: put the victim's feelings and needs in priority over an apprehension; use basic and non-technical words; be cognizant of one's voice, tone and posture when asking questions; ask her to lock the windows and doors prior to the arrival of help; and ask her to wrap in something warm to avoid shock (but not change her clothes). The "don'ts" include: not to change clothes or change her appearance; not to drink, eat or cleanse; and not to touch anything unnecessarily. The items in the "don't" list ensure preservation of physical evidence for adjudication. Often, the victim's initial reaction is to shower in an attempt to "wash herself clean" of the assault. Precautions to preserve physical evidence are described in detail in Johnson (1985).

CONCLUSION

The fact that date rape happens to a large number of women on campuses holds many implications for administrators. It seems of primary importance that the offices having significant contact with students receive training to enable them to recognize symptoms of date rape as well as inform them as to when and where to make referrals. Administrators need to learn how to conduct thorough inquiries which, at the same time, will not increase the sense of intrusion and invasion experienced by many victims. One cannot emphasize enough the importance of conducting training programs which will enable administrators and victims to feel at ease with the difficult and highly emotional issue of date rape and sexual assault.

APPENDIX A
WHAT IS DATE/
ACQUAINTANCE RAPE?*

Date/acquaintance rape is the act of forced and coerced sex. It is sexual violence against women and is not associated with love or lust. Examples of a date/acquaintance rapist include a date, classmate, friend, study partner, friend of a friend or floor mate. Date/acquaintance rape may not be recognized to be "real rape" by the victim, the attacker or the victim's friends and family; a rape does not have to be committed by a stranger hiding behind a bush. Most date/acquaintance rapes are committed by seemingly "nice guys" whom the woman may know.

CAN IT HAPPEN TO ME?

Date/acquaintance rape can happen to anyone, any time, any place. Women between the ages of 16 and 24 are at greatest risk of becoming victims. Here are some facts:

- 33% to 54% of female college students revealed some form of sexual victimization,

- 25% of male college students admitted to engaging in some form of sexual aggression,

- 48% of students knew at least one victim,

- 7% of victims talked to a counselor,

- 80% of victims self-disclosed to friends,

- 37% of victims confided in relatives.

Date/acquaintance rape can occur on campuses in suburban, rural and urban areas; at private and public colleges; at ivy league, city and state universities; and at 2-year and community colleges. Most rapes occur in the residence of the attacker or the victim or in an isolated area such as a parked car, beach or park. Loud music is typically played to muffle sounds. Alcohol and/or drug use by the attacker and/or the victim is reported in over half of reported incidents.

---

*Compiled from information used by SAVES 5/91.

WHAT CAN I DO TO PREVENT DATE/ACQUAINTANCE RAPE?

For Men

Accept the Woman's Decision. "No" means "no." Don't read other meanings into it.

Don't Assume That You Can Coerce the Woman Because: *You paid* for the evening . . . *She agreed to hook up* and changed her mind . . . *You picked her up* at a party . . . *You've had sex* with her before . . . *You think women enjoy being coerced* or "persuaded" into sex . . . *She dressed in a "sexy" manner* and flirted with you . . .

Being Turned Down When You Ask for Sex is Not Personal Rejection. Women who say "No" to sex are not rejecting the person; they are expressing their desire not to participate in an act. Your desires may be beyond your control but your actions are within your control.

For Women

Know Basic Information About Your Date. Know his full name and where he lives. Tell others where you expect to be, with whom and when you expect to return.

Avoid Isolated and/or Dangerous Places. Initially get to know him in a group environment or public setting rather than as a couple.

Be Aware of Your Nonverbal Actions. Nonverbal messages are sent by your posture, voice, gestures and eye contact. They may be unintentional or may contradict verbal messages. Make both messages consistent.

Pay Attention to What Is Happening Around You. Don't put yourself in vulnerable situations. Watch the nonverbal cues.

Be Assertive. Be direct and firm when sexually pressured.

Trust Your Intuitions. If you feel pressured into sex, you probably are.

For Everyone

Know Your Sexual Desires and Limits. Communicate them clearly. Before you get into a sexual situation, make your limits clear. For women, say "no" when you mean "no" and don't let others violate your personal space. For men, be aware of social pressure to "score;" it's OK not to "score."

Avoid Excessive Use of Alcohol and Drugs. Chemical substances interfere with clear thinking, judgment and effective communication.

Use common sense for personal safety.

Educate Others. Plan class projects, speeches and term papers on date/acquaintance rape or sexual assault. Maintain a bulletin board on your residence floor or door to post information. Encourage others to assist and make it a floor, hall or class project.

Volunteer for or Establish a Sexual Assault Program on Campus or in the Community. Become a peer educator. Sponsor a sexual assault awareness week.

Know How to Help a Victim and How to Get Assistance. Be familiar with campus resources such as Campus Police, Health Services, Counseling Services, Women's Center and Sexual Assault Program. Encourage the victim to seek assistance and to report the incident to the Judicial Officer and/or Campus Police.

Keep Sexual Assault/Domestic Violence Hotline Number Accessible • 800-333-SAFE.

Start a Date/Acquaintance Rape Support Group on Campus.

APPENDIX B
ORIENTATION AND PRE-SERVICE
TRAINING PROGRAM

I. Training Sessions

Training will take place on eight evenings and two Saturdays for a total of 40 hours.

Session 1:   ***Introduction to Sexual Assault***

(3 hours)
- Introduction of Staff
- Tour of Agency
- Statistics
- Myths and Facts
- Patterns of Rape
- Domestic Violence and Sexual Assault
- Date Rape
- Marital Rape
- Profile of Rapists

Session 2:   ***Introduction of the Rape Crisis Program***

(3 hours)
- Purpose of the Rape Crisis Program
- Policies and Procedures
- Confidentiality
- Policies Concerning Minors
- Job Description for Volunteers
- Expectations of Volunteers

Session 3:   ***Medical Information***

(8 hours)
- The Rape Examination
- Working with the Hospital Staff
- Tour of the Hospital
- HIV Infection
- Sexually Transmitted Disease (STDs)
- Morning After Pill (DES)

Session 4:   *Legal Information*

(3 hours)
- Laws about Sexual Assault
- Victim's Legal Options
- What Happens if the Victim Prosecutes: The Criminal Justice System
- The Rape Victim in Court
- Victim-Witness Program
- Child Sexual Assault Victim Advocate

Session 5:   Psychological Impact on Victim and Victim's Friends and Family

(3 hours)
- Rape Trauma Syndrome
- Victim's Reactions to Rape
- Counseling the Adult Female
- Counseling Gay/Lesbian, Minors, Male and Third World Victims

Session 6:   Referrals

(3 hours)
- Needs Identification
- Recognizing the Illicit/Prescription Drug User
- Alcohol Involvement in Sexual Assault
- Discussion of Various Agencies for Referrals
- When and How to Make Referrals

Session 7:   Counseling

(8 hours)
- Role Playing
- Values Clarification Exercises
- Therapy Versus Support
- Basic Counseling Techniques
- Crisis Intervention Skills: Hotline Calls and Initial Interview
- Listening Techniques

Session 8:   Child Victims

(3 hours)
- Adults Molested as Children (AMACS)
- Child Sexual Abuse Prevention Program

Session 9:   Self-defense Techniques

(3 hours)
- How to Make the Victim Feel Safe Again
- Self-defense Demonstration

Session 10:   ***Public Speaking***

(3 hours)   • Stress and Anger Management for Counselors working with Victims of Sexual Assault

    • Presentation and Public Speaking Styles

II.   Individual Session

Each student meets for one to two hours with the supervisor to discuss problems, concerns, questions and/or willingness or suitability for the field placement.

APPENDIX C
MYTHS AND FACTS QUIZ

by Juneau Mahan Gary & Karen Calabria Briskin

The following quiz has been successful in increasing audience participation by providing structure for group discussion of an emotionally-laden issue. The quiz encourages workshop participants to examine their beliefs in a supportive and informative environment by committing them to choosing an answer, thus making it difficult for them to remain neutral or silent. The quiz should be administered at the beginning of a workshop to enable the presenter(s) to ascertain the group's level and to gear the workshop accordingly.

Answers accompany each question with a brief explanation of salient points. The explanations are intended to be illustrative rather than exhaustive in scope. The explanations are presented in lay terms for easier comprehension.

Directions: This quiz is intended to explore your knowledge about sexual assault. It is an instrument for discussion only. It is not scored; you cannot fail. Read the statements below and decide which are myths and which are facts by marking "M" for myth and "F" for fact. Please take no more than ten minutes to complete.

1. _____ **The primary motive for rape is sexual.**

Myth. The motive for rape is aggression and power; not sex. Rapists have a desire to dominate, humiliate and degrade their victims. Rape is not the result of "pent up" sexual desire, for many offenders report that they do not enjoy the sex act *per se* during rape. In fact, most offenders have access to a sexual relationship with a wife or lover.

2. _____ **Women are sexually assaulted because they "ask for it" in some way.**

Myth. Attempts to shift the burden of blame from the offender to the victim by implying that "she asked for it" are common. Being a victim has no connection to one's dress or "provocative" manner. The shift of blame directs attention to the victim and away from the offender, thereby absolving or diminishing the offender's responsibility for the attack.

3. _____ **Sexual assaults are usually planned.**

Fact. Most sexual assaults are planned in advance by the offender. The act is premeditated but the specific victim tends to be chosen at random based on her availability and vulnerability.

"I'm not raping a person, just any woman — it doesn't make any difference who she is," illustrates a common attitude among rapists.

4. _____ **Sexual assault cannot happen to a respectable woman.**

Myth. Any woman can be sexually assaulted, regardless of her age, appearance, social status or race.

5. _____ **A woman can nearly always prevent an assault by resisting her attacker.**

Myth. Every sexual assault is unique and the issue of resistance and submission should be evaluated individually. Resistance could deter an attack, or it could conceivably increase one's chances of injury and perhaps result in death. The victim needs to do whatever she must to extricate herself from the situation while considering the following variables: the element of surprise, the offender's probable greater size or strength and the possibility of a weapon. The victim should rely on her instincts, and whatever she does to survive is correct *for her.* Even if she must submit, this does not imply consent and, in fact, may keep her alive.

6. _____ **Men cannot be sexually assaulted.**

Myth. Men can be, and are, sexually assaulted. Male sexual assault is estimated to be about two percent of reported assaults. Nearly always, men are assaulted by other men. When assaulted, men tend not to report the assault as frequently as women do. Instead, they use coping styles to avoid or circumvent the dilemmas of reporting and prosecuting that are experienced by women. These coping styles enable them to escape the additional trauma of others doubting their sexual orientation and help to repress their fears and concerns about their own masculinity and sexual preference.

7. _____ **Most women actually enjoy rape.**

Myth. Most women enjoy consensual sexual relationships and rape is not consensual. A woman's "seduction" fantasy is frequently confused with the supposed enjoyment of rape. In the seduction fantasy, the woman is completely in control of her scenario, actions and actors. Violence or abuse is seldom part of the fantasy. During a sexual assault, however, the woman is not in control of the violence, abuse, events or her body. In fact, victims report that the primary emotions they felt during the attack were fear for their lives, humiliation, intimidation and degradation.

8. _____ **Most reported sexual assaults are true.**

Fact. Reported sexual assaults are true, with very few exceptions. FBI crime statistics indicate the false report rate for assaults to be only two percent; this is similar to the false report of other major crime reports. The general misconception of a high rate of false reports of sexual assaults may be confused with observations of low conviction rates of offenders. Low conviction rates are not caused by high rates of false reports. They are caused by other factors including insufficient evidence to prosecute, dismissal of trial due to technicalities and the reluctance of victims to testify.

9. _____ **Many assaults are committed by an offender known to the victim.**

Fact. The victim is acquainted with her offender in more than half of reported sexual assaults. For example, many victims tend not to report an assault by a family member, lover, date or acquaintance under the mistaken belief that only assaults committed by strangers are sexual offenses and consequently punishable. Other reasons for the reluctance to report this type of assault include feelings of ambivalence toward the offender and concern about problematic prosecution. The previously established relationship between victim and offender tends to raise doubts and to elicit less sympathy from some juries than an assault by a stranger. Society is less likely to acknowledge a date rape because of preconceived notions and myths about "real" rape and traditional sex role stereotypes (e.g., she says "no" when she means "yes"). These suppositions are reinforced through the media and by cultural images concerning sexual interaction.

10. _____ **Most parents who sexually abuse their children have a history of sexual abuse, physical abuse or neglect during their own childhood.**

Fact. Many factors are involved in the sexual abuse of children. One of the most common factors is a history of abuse in a parent's background. Abusive parents have an incidence of prior sexual or physical abuse much greater than that of the general population. Many incidents of child sexual abuse remain undisclosed until adulthood. The victim may confide in someone during his or her college years.

11. _____ **Most sexual assaults are interracial.**

Myth. Most sexual assaults take place between members of the same race. White victims tend to report Black offenders more frequently than White offenders, and Black victims tend to under-report assaults in general, but especially if the offender is White. Black offenders tend to be convicted in disproportionately higher numbers based on arrest rates. The myth that Black men rape only White women may be perpetuated by the publicity given to those assaults fitting cultural and racial stereotypes.

12. _____ **Rape is not a big deal; it's only sex.**

Myth. Rape is a big deal; it is illegal and punishable. It is not committed between consenting adults, but is forced and violent. Rape victims report having more in common with victims of other serious crimes such as physical assault, burglary and attempted murder than with partners in a consensual sexual relationship. Victims report stressful feelings such as loss of control, physical violation and invasion of privacy.

13. _____ **The younger the victim, the more likely that the offender is well-known to the family or is a family member.**

Fact. As children, victims are taught to trust family members and close friends. Abusing adults violate the trust of younger victims. Children should be encouraged to follow their "gut" feelings in uncomfortable situations. They need to be taught the differences between "good" and "bad" touches and to be encouraged to say "no" to inappropriate suggestions and behavior.

14. _____ **Most sexual assaults are not reported to the police.**

Fact. Although estimates of reported sexual assaults vary, sources agree that a very low percentage is actually reported. The Law Enforcement Assistance Administration (LEAA) estimates that there are 3.36 sexual assaults committed for each one reported. In one study, only eight percent of the women who were assaulted filed reports. Based on these statistics, one can conclude that sexual assaults remain unreported and under-reported to a vast degree.

15. _____ **HIV (Human Immunodeficiency Virus) infection can be transmitted during a sexual assault.**

Fact. HIV (Human Immunodeficiency Virus) is the virus transmitting AIDS and is exchanged from one person to another through infected blood or semen. HIV can enter a victim's body through a tear in the wall of the anus, vagina or mouth cavity. A victim will usually know little or none of the offender's past sexual history, his experience with intravenous (IV) drug use or his HIV status. Some states are conducting HIV testing for convicted sex offenders and are conveying the results of the tests to respective victims. A positive HIV test does not mean that the victim will get AIDS; it means HIV antigens are present and the body is producing antibodies.

16. _____ **Most sexual assault victims react hysterically.**

Myth. Individual reactions to a sexual assault are as varied as the individuals themselves. Reactions may appear immediately or may be delayed. One's response to an event depends on many factors including personality, experiences with similar events in the past, intensity of the event and reactions of others. Victims' reactions can range from hysteria to calm and rational behavior, but the majority of victims appear stunned and bewildered. Reports from women who reacted in a calm, rational manner often felt discounted because they did not exhibit stereotypical "female" hysteria and were suspected of making a false allegation.

17. _____ **A woman's past sexual history is usually admissible in a sexual assault trial.**

Myth. A woman's past sexual history is usually not admissible in court due to "shield" laws. One exception, however, may be if there was a prior sexual relationship between the victim and the attacker (e.g., former boyfriend). In the past, the woman's prior sexual history was used to displace attention from the offender and onto the victim. Now the trial is based on the offender's behavior.

18. _____ **A victim can withdraw from the prosecution process at any time.**

Fact. The victim, after filing a complaint, cannot be forced to pursue the prosecution by the District Attorney/Prosecutor, police, family or anyone else.

19. _____ **Only the young or beautiful may be sexually assaulted.**

Myth. Victims range in age from a few months to 90 years old and come in all shapes, sizes and colors. Victims tend to be chosen for their perceived vulnerability and availability, without regard to their physical appearance. Attributing a sexual assault to a victim's attractiveness perpetuates the myth that a rape is primarily motivated by sexual desire. This myth inappropriately places blame and responsibility onto the victim because of her physical attributes.

20. _____ **Many women "cry rape" to protect their reputation or to seek revenge against a lover.**

Myth. False reports of rapes are rare and reported to be only two percent. Most women would not volunteer to disclose publicly the intimate details of a sexual assault if the event did not occur.

21. _____ **Sexual assault only occurs in dark alleys and isolated areas.**

Myth. A sexual assault can happen anywhere and at any time. In fact, surprisingly high numbers of assaults occur in places ordinarily thought to be safe, like homes, cars, residence halls and offices. Often, a rapist will manipulate a victim to gain access to a "safe" place because this location reduces his chances of being observed and subsequently apprehended. Also, women tend to avoid stereotypically dangerous situations such as dark alleys and isolated areas; hence, higher proportions of assaults happen in "safe" places than one would expect.

22. _____ **Most assaults happen during summer months.**

Fact. Statistics indicate that sexual assaults tend to increase during warmer months and to decrease during the colder months. For example, New Jersey Uniform Crime Reports statistics indicated that the highest number of reported sexual assaults consistently occur during July and August. On campuses, though, statistics indicate the opposite because students are on campus from September to May. September and April/May are the highest incidence months on campus.

23. _____ **The physician, after examination of the victim, determines if a sexual assault has occurred.**

Myth. Sexual assault is a *legal* definition rather than a medical definition. The judgment of sexual assault is made in a court of law. Physicians furnish medical reports and impressions to the court for ruling. Physicians do not have the legal authority to decide if the victim was assaulted. Regardless of the legal decision, however, if the victim perceives herself as having been assaulted, the experience is a traumatic event in her life and should be treated as such.

24. _____ **An adult cannot ignore the suspected sexual or physical abuse of a child.**

Fact. Anyone who suspects or can confirm the sexual or physical abuse of a child is required, under law in every state, to report such an incident. Courts have held physicians, in particular, liable for damages which occurred to a child after the physician failed to report an abusive family situation.

25. _____ **A woman cannot be raped by her husband.**

Myth. This myth has its roots in the antiquated concept that a woman is the private property of her husband and is consequently at his sexual disposal. Although the laws vary, marital rape is now a criminal offense in almost half of the states. However, this remains the most difficult type of sexual assault to prove.

MYTH/FACT QUIZ ABOUT SEXUAL ASSAULT
(Condensed Version)

1. _____ The primary motive for rape is sexual.

2. _____ Women are sexually assaulted because they "ask for it" in some way.

3. _____ Sexual assaults are usually planned.

4. _____ Sexual assault cannot happen to a respectable woman.

5. _____ A woman can prevent an assault by resisting her attacker.

6. _____ Men cannot be sexually assaulted.

7. _____ Most women actually enjoy rape.

8. _____ Most reported sexual assaults are true.

9. _____ Many assaults are committed by an offender known to the victim.

10. _____ Most parents who sexually abuse their children have a history of sexual abuse, physical abuse and/or neglect during their own childhood.

11. _____ Most sexual assaults are interracial.

12. _____ Rape is not a big deal; it's only sex.

13. _____ The younger the victim, the more likely that the offender is well-known to the family or is a family member.

14. _____ Most sexual assaults are not reported to the police.

15. _____ HIV (Human Immunodeficiency Virus) infection can be transmitted during a sexual assault.

16. _____ Most sexual assault victims react hysterically.

17. _____ A woman's past sexual history is admissible in a sexual assault trial.

18. _____ A victim can withdraw from the prosecution process at any time.

19. _____ Only the young or beautiful may be sexually assaulted.

20. _____ Many women "cry rape" to protect their reputation or to seek revenge against a lover.

21. _____ Sexual assault only occurs in dark alleys and isolated areas.

22. _____ Most assaults occur during summer months.

23. _____ The physician, after examination of the victim, determines if a sexual assault has occurred.

24. _____ An adult cannot ignore the suspected sexual and/or physical abuse of a child.

25. _____ A woman cannot be raped by her husband.

APPENDIX D
IF YOU ARE RAPED:
DO'S AND DON'TS

DO

- Get help *immediately* and tell someone.

- Get to a safe place or lock windows and doors until identified help arrives.

- Call a support person (i.e., rape crisis counselor or a friend, relative or spouse).

- Wrap loosely in something warm to avoid shock (but do not remove clothing).

DON'T

- Change clothes or appearance.

- Eat, drink, cleanse or eliminate bodily waste.

- Touch anything unnecessarily.

Recommended reading: *If You Are Raped*, K. Johnson, 1985.

APPENDIX E
IF SHE IS RAPED: DO'S AND DON'TS
FOR SIGNIFICANT OTHERS*

DO

- Encourage her to seek medical treatment, request crisis counseling, ask for a support person and file a police and campus judicial report.

- Give her the opportunity to re-establish her feelings of control and ability to make decisions.

- Assist her in making decisions, if she requests.

- Be sensitive to her need for privacy.

- Verbally express your anger about the incident and the offender, but not toward her.

- Be patient, understanding and approachable.

- Create a safe, supportive and accepting atmosphere for her to discuss painful feelings and her reactions and fears.

- Be alert to changes in her appetite, quality of social interactions, sleep patterns, study habits, thoughts of suicide or homicide, fear of being alone, and emotional stability. Get professional help as appropriate.

- Encourage her to resume her regular lifestyle as soon as possible.

- Attend to recurring themes in her conversation.

- Identify a support person for you to ventilate feelings so you can be available for her.

*Significant others are friends, roommates, lovers, acquaintances, relatives, spouses, and children of the victim.

DON'T

- Let her do anything to destroy evidence or make changes at the scene of the assault. Perhaps physically small but significant pieces of evidence (e.g., clothing fibers, hair strands, mucous, saliva) may be destroyed.

- Doubt her story or be critical or judgemental.

- Pressure her to talk about the incident until she feels ready. Just let her know you are available to talk when she is comfortable.

- Demand, pressure or request sexual activity too soon following the assault. Take cues from her.

- Be angry with her.

- Attempt a vengeful act against the offender. Threats of revenge are counter-productive and physical aggression should not be pursued.

- Blame the victim or encourage her to blame herself.

- Overprotect or limit her independence or hover too closely. You want to convey support, not smothering or dependence.

- Spread gossip.

Recommended reading: *If She is Raped,* A. McEvoy & J. Brookings, 1991.

SAMPLE TRENTON STATE COLLEGE*
SEXUAL ASSAULT VICTIM EDUCATION AND
SUPPORT-UNIT (SAVES-U) NEWSLETTER
SPRING 1993

(609) 771-3211 (24-hour Hotline on Campus)
(609) 771-2247 • 989-9332 (24-hour Hotline off Campus)
Monday-Friday • 8:30-4:30

PROS AND CONS OF REPORTING SEXUAL ASSAULT

Some sexual assault victims do not report the offense immediately. However, a late report is better than no report at all. Reporting a sexual assault to the police means that you can be helped as soon as possible. It does not mean that you must press charges. However, if you do decide later to press charges, the necessary evidence and information will have been collected.

Pros . . .

- If you report the crime and the rapist is caught, you may have protected others.

- You might be eligible for financial compensation through the State.

- You are exercising your rights.

- It's a step in your recovery process.

Cons . . .

- You will have to repeat your story to the police and prosecutor.

---

*Reprinted, in part, from *People Against Rape.*

- The prosecutor will decide if your case will go to trial. If it does not, you have the right to know why your case was not filed.

- Only one in five cases make it to court. Of those that do, there is a high conviction rate.

- All this might be emotionally difficult for you.

Should You Report?

If you do not wish to prosecute your assailant, this is your privilege. You will be given a physical examination at the hospital, if you wish, then you will be sent home.

If you have not been accompanied by a police officer to the hospital and wish to report the incident, the police will be called for you. Feel free to ask questions and voice your concerns to the officer.

Get Help On Campus

Assistance is available on campus. Report an assault to **Campus Police (x2345)**, get medical attention at **Hamilton Hospital (584-6666),** get routine medical assistance from **Health Services (x2483, 107 Community Commons), Women's Center (x2120),** report it to the **judicial officer in the Dean of Student Life Office (x2201, Brower Student Center)**, get counseling at **Psychological Counseling Services (x2247, 107 Community Commons),** contact the **SAVES hotline (x3211),** call the **Rape Crisis hotline (989-9332 or x3211),** ask a friend to accompany you if you feel uncomfortable.

(For additional samples, please call SAVES-U at 609-771-2247.)

APPENDIX G
REFERENCES AND
SUGGESTED READINGS

Abbey, A. (1991). "Acquaintance rape and alcohol consumption on college campuses: How are they linked?" *Journal of American College Health, 39* (4), 165-169.

Adams, A. & Abarbanel, G. (1988). *Sexual assault on campus: What colleges can do.* Santa Monica, CA: Santa Monica Rape Treatment Center.

Adams, C., Fay, J. & Loreen-Martin, J. (1984). *No is not enough: Helping teenagers avoid sexual assault.* San Luis Obispo, CA: Impact Publishers.

Aizenman, M. & Kelly G. (1988). "The incidence of violence and acquaintance rape in dating relationships among college men and women," *Journal of College Student Development, 29,* 305-311.

Amir, M. (1971). *Patterns of forcible rape.* Chicago, IL: University of Chicago Press.

American Health Care Association. (1976). *Establishing and maintaining a volunteer program.* Washington, DC: American Health Care Association (1200 15th St., N.W., Washington, DC).

Auvine, B., Densmore, B., Extrom, M., Poole, S. & Shanklin, M. (1978). *A manual for group facilitators.* Madison, WI: Center for Conflict Resolution.

Baier, J., Rosenzweig, M. & Whipple, E. (1991). "Patterns of sexual behavior, coercion and victimization of university students," *Journal of College Student Development, 32,* 310-322.

Bart, P.B. & O'Brien, P.H. (1985). *Stopping rape: Successful survival strategies.* Elmsford, NY: Pergamon Press.

Beneke, T. (1983). *Men on rape: What they have to say about sexual violence.* New York: St. Martin.

Benson, D., Charlton, C. & Goodhart, F. (1992). "Acquaintance rape on campus: A literature review," *Journal of American College Health, 40,* (4), 157-165.

Benson, B. (1992). "The public safety 'sexual assault guarantee' at Michigan State University," *Campus Law Enforcement Journal,* Nov-Dec, 26-28.

Braen, G.R. "The male rape victim: Examination and management." In C.G. Warner (Ed.) (1980). *Rape and sexual assault: Management and intervention.* Germantown, MD: Aspen Publication.

Bridges, J. (1991). "Perceptions of date and stranger rape: A difference in sex role expectations and rape-supportive beliefs," *Sex Roles,* 24(5/6), 291-307.

Briskin, K.C. & Gary, J.M. (1986). "Sexual assault programming for college students," *Journal of Counseling and Development,* 65, 207-208.

Brownmiller, S. (1975). *Against our will: Men, women and rape.* New York: Bantam Books.

Bureau of Justice Statistics (1985). *The crime of rape.* Washington, DC: U.S. Department of Justice.

Burgess, A.W. & Holmstrom, L.L. (Eds.). (1979). *Rape: Crisis and recovery.* Bowie, MD: Robert J. Brady Co.

Burgess, A.W. & Holmstrom, L.L. (1988). "Treating the adult rape victim," *Medical Aspects of Human Sexuality,* 36-44.

Burkhart, B. (1983). *Acquaintance rape statistics and prevention.* Paper presented at the Acquaintance Rape and Rape Prevention on Campus Conference, Louisville, KY.

Burling, P. (1991). *Crime on campus: Analyzing and managing the increasing risk of institutional liability.* Washington, DC: National Association of College and University Attorneys.

Burt, M.R. (1980). "Cultural myths and support for rape," *Journal of Personality and Social Psychology,* 38, 217-230.

Byington, D.B. & Keeter, K.W. (1988). "Assessing needs of sexual assault victims on a university campus." In *Student services: Responding to issues and challenges.* Chapel Hill, NC: The University of North Carolina General Administration.

Cannel, J.M., (1989). *Title 2C New Jersey code of criminal justice* (with comments and annotations). Newark, NJ: Gann Law Books.

Carrow, D.M. (1980). *Rape: Guidelines for a community response.* Washington, DC: National Institute for Law Enforcement and Criminal Justice, U.S. Department of Justice.

Clark, L. & Lewis, D. (1977). *Rape: The price of coercive sexuality.* Toronto, Canada: The Women's Press.

Egidio, R.K. & Robertson, D.E. (1981). "Rape awareness for men," *Journal of College Student Personnel,* Sept., 455-456.

Ehrhart, J.K. & Sandler, B.R. (1985). *Campus gang rape: Party games?* Washington, DC: Project on the Status and Education of Women, Association of Women, Association of American Colleges.

Enos, W.F. & Beyer, J.C. (1978). "Management of the rape victim," *American Family Practice,* 18, (3), 97-102.

Federal Bureau of Investigation. (1989). *Uniform crime reports for the United States,* 1988. Washington, DC: Government Printing Office.

Federal Bureau of Investigation. (1986). *Crime in the United States: Uniform crime reports.* Washington, DC: Department of Justice.

Fiesta, J. (1983). *The law and liability - A guide for nurses.* New York: John Wiley and Sons.

Ford, R.D. & Haston, L. (Eds.). (1985). *Nurse's Legal Handbook.* Pennsylvania: Springhouse Corporation.

Fortune, M. (1984). *Sexual assault prevention: A study for teenagers.* New York: United Church Press.

Friedman, D. (1979). "Rape, racism and reality," *Quest,* 1979, 40-51.

Goodwin, J. (1982). *Sexual assault: Incest victims and their families.* Boston, MA: John Wright, Inc.

Griffin, S. (1971). "Rape: The all-American crime," *Ramparts,* September, 26-35.

Gordon, M.T. & Riger, S. (1989). *The female fear.* New York: Free Press.

Greensite, G. (1984). *Resources against sexual assault.* Santa Cruz, CA: Rape Prevention Education Program, University of California-Santa Cruz.

Groth, A.N. (1979). *Men who rape: The psychology of the offender.* New York: Plenum Press.

Groth, A.N. & Burgess, W. (1980). "Male rape: Offenders and victims," *American Journal of Psychiatry,* 137, 806-810.

Hatcher, R., Atkinson, A., Cates, D., Glasser, L. & Legins, K. (1992). *Sexual ettiquette 101.* Atlanta, GA: Bridging the Gap Comminications, Inc.

Harris, R.A. (1985). *How to select, train and use volunteers in hospitals, homes and agencies.* Springfield, IL: Charles C. Thomas.

Hicks, D.J. (1980). "Rape: Sexual assault," *American Journal of Obstetrics and Gynecology,* 137, 931-935.

Hilberman, E. (1976). *The rape victim.* Baltimore, MD: Garamond/Pridemark Press.

Hodge, M. & Blyskal, J. (1989). "Who says college campuses are safe?" *Readers Digest,* March, 14-30.

Hughes, J.O., O'Gorman, J. & Sanlder, B.R. (1987). *Friends raping friends: Could it happen to you?* Washington, D.C.: Project on the Status and Education of Women, Association of American Colleges.

Hyde, M.O. (1987). *Sexual assault: Let's talk about it.* Philadelphia, PA: Westminster Press.

Johnson, K.M. (1985). *If you are raped.* Holmes Beach, FL: Learning Publications, Inc.

Journal of American College Health. (1992). *Violence on campus: The changing faces of college health* (Special Issue), 40(4).

Journal of American College Health. (1993). *Research perspectives on campus violence,* (Special Issue), 40(4).

Kanin, E.J. & Parcell, S.R. (1977). "Sexual aggression: A second look at the offended female," *Archives of Sexual Behavior,* 6, 67-76.

Katz, J.H. (1984). *No fairy godmothers, no magic wands: The healing process after rape.* Saratoga, CA: R and E Publishers.

Kaufman, A., Divasto, P., Jackson, R., Voorhees, D. & Christy, J. (1980). "Male rape victim: Noninstitutionalized assault," *American Journal of Psychiatry,* 137, 221-223.

Keefe, J.E. (1985). *Mbonte v Rutgers,* Middlesex County (NJ).

Keller, D. (1992). *Rape . . . Awareness, education, prevention and response: A practical guide for college and university administrators.* Goshen, KY: Campus Crime Prevention Programs.

Koss, M.P. & Oros, C.J. (1982). "Sexual experiences survey: A research instrument investigating sexual aggression and victimization," *Journal of Consulting and Clinical Psychology,* 50, 455-457.

Koss, M.P., Leonard, K.E., Breezley, D.A. & Oros, C.J. (1985). "Non-stranger sexual aggression: A discriminant analysis of the psychological characteristics of undetected offenders," *Sex Roles,* 12, 981-992.

Koss, M.P., Gidycz, C.A. & Wisniewski, N. (1987). "The scope of rape: Incidence and prevalence of sexual aggression and victimization in a national sample of higher educaiton students," *Journal of Consulting and Clinical Psychology,* 55, (2), 162-170.

Koss, M.P. & Harvey, M.R. (1991). *The rape victim: Clinical and community interventions.* Newbury Park, CA: Sage Publications.

Krauss, P. & Goldfischer, M. (1988). *Why me? Coping with grief, loss and change.* New York: Bantam Books.

Kubler-Ross, E. (1969). *On death and dying.* New York: Macmillan Publishing.

Kushner, H.S. (1981). *When bad things happen to good people.* New York: Schocken Books.

Landau, S.I. (Ed.). (1966). *Funk and Wagnalls standard college dictionary.* New York: Reader's Digest Books, Inc.

Larsen, E. & Hagerty, C.L. (1992). *From anger to forgiveness.* Center City, MN: Hazeldon Educational Materials.

Law Enforcement Assistance Administration. (1975). *Criminal victimization surveys in eight American cities.* Washington, DC: U.S. Government Printing Office.

"Lawsuit charges mishandling of rape cases." (1991b, April 7). *New York Times* (Campus Life Section), P. 40.

Ledray, L.E. (1986) *Recovering from rape.* New York, NY: Henry Holt and Co.

Lee, L.A. (1987). "Rape prevention: Experiential training for men," *Journal of Counseling and Development,* 66, 100-101.

Lobb, C. (1976). *Exploring careers through volunteerism.* New York: Richards Rosen Press.

Long, N.T. (1985). "The standard of proof in student disciplinary cases," *Journal of College and University Law,* 12(1).

Maletzky, B.M. (1980). "Self-referred vs. court-referred sexually deviant patients: Success with assisted covert sensitization," *Behavior Therapy,* 11, 306-314.

McCahill, T.W., Meyer, L.C. & Fischman, A.M. (1979). *The aftermath of rape.* Toronto, Canada: Lexington Books.

Mccombie, S.L. (Ed.). (1980). The rape crisis intervention handbook. New York: Plenum Press.

McEvoy, A. & Brookings, J. (1991). *If she is raped: A Guidebook for husbands, fathers and male friends* (2nd ed.). Holmes Beach, FL: Learning Publications.

Miller, E. (1981). "Preventing acquaintance rape," *WOARPATH, 7*(11), 9-10.

Mills, P. (Ed.). (1977). *Rape intervention resource manual.* Springfield, IL: Charles C. Thomas.

Muehlenhard, C.L. & Linton, M.A. (1987). "Date rape and sexual aggression in dating situations: Incident and risk factors," *Journal of Counseling Psychology, 34,* (2), 186-196.

Naylor, H.H. (1976). *Leadership for volunteering.* Dryden, NY: Dryden Associates.

N.O.W./Legal Defense and Education Fund & Cherow-O'Leary, R. (1987). *The state-by-state guide to women's legal rights.* New York: McGraw-Hill.

O'Reilly, D. (1990, October 18). "Few colleges file reports: Fear of bad publicity discourages disclosure," *Philadelphia Inquirer,* p. E1.

Parrot, A. & Link, R. (1983). *Acquaintance rape in a college population.* Paper presented at the Eastern Regional Conference of the Society for the Scientific Study of Sex, Philadelphia, PA.

Parrot, A. (1988). *Acquaintance rape and sexual assault prevention training manual,* 3rd. Edition. Ithaca, NY: Cornell University, College of Human Ecology, Department of Human Service Studies.

Parrot, A. (1988). *Coping with date rape and acquaintance rape.* New York: Rosen Publishing Group.

Porter, E. (1986). *Treating the young male victims of sexual assault: Issues and intervention strategies.* Syracuse, NY: Safer Society Press.

Pritchard, C. (1988). *Avoiding rape on and off campus.* Glassboro, NJ: State College Publishing Co.

Quinsey, V. (1984). "Sexual aggression: Studies of offenders against women." In D.N. Weisstaub (Ed.) *Law and mental health: International perspectives,* Vol. 1, New York: Pergamon.

Rada, R.T. (1975a). "Alcohol and rape," *Medical Aspects of Human Sexuality,* 2, 48-65.

Rada, R.T. (1975b). "Alcoholism and forcible rape," *American Journal of Psychiatry,* 132, 444-446.

Rapaport, K. & Burkhart, B.R. (1984). "Personality and attitudinal characteristics of sexually coercive college males," *Journal of Abnormal Psychology,* 93, 216-221.

Rencken, R.H. (1989). *Intervention strategies for sexual assault.* Alexandria, VA: American Association for Counseling and Development.

Roark, M.L. (1985). "Task force on victimization and violence on campus," *American College Personnel Association Developments,* XIII, 15.

Roark, M.L. (1987). "Preventing violence on college campuses," *Journal of Counseling and Development,* 65, 367-371.

Russell, D. (1982). *Rape in marriage.* Beverly Hills, CA: Sage Publications.

Russell, D.E. (1984). *Sexual exploitation: Rape, child sexual abuse and workplace harassment.* Beverly Hills, CA: Sage Publications.

Scacco, A.M. (Ed.). (1982). *Male rape.* New York: AMS Press.

Scheppele, K.L. & Bart, P.B. (1983). "Through women's eyes: Defining danger in the wake of sexual assault," *Journal of Social Issues,* 39, (2), 63-80.

Shearer, S.L. & Herbert, C.A. (1987). "Long-term effects of unresolved sexual trauma," *American Family Practice,* 36, (4), 169-175.

Smith, J.W. (1975). "Commentary on alcohol and rape," *Medical Aspects of Human Sexuality,* 2, 60-62.

Staff. (1993). *Statement concerning campus disciplinary procedures and the criminal law in sexual assault cases.* Washington, D.C.: National Association of Student Personnel Administrators (NASPA).

Staff. (1985). *The problem of rape on campus.* Washington, DC: Project on the Status and Education of Women, Association of American Colleges.

Steinman, M. (1987). "Arrest policies and spouse abuse: Putting new policy directions in perspective," *American Journal of Police* VI (2), 11-26.

Stevens, M. (1988). "Standing committee on campus violence," *American College Personnel Association Developments,* XV, 3.

"Student's date-rape complaint jolts William and Mary: Criticism of administration's reaction has campus confronting difficult issues" (1991, April 4). *Washington Post,* p.B1.

Task force seeks revised handling of rape cases, (1991a, February 10). *New York Times* (Campus Life Section), p. 49.

Tatelbaum, J. (1980). *The courage to grieve.* New York: Harper and Rowe.

Turetsky, J. (1981). "Marital rape and the law," *WOARPATH,* 7, (11), 4-5.

Uniform Crime Report Unit. (1988). *Crime in New Jersey.* West Trenton: State of New Jersey, Division of State Police.

Warner, C.G. (Ed.). (1980). *Rape and sexual assault.* Germantown, MD: Aspen Publication.

Warshaw, R. (1988). *I never called it rape.* Scranton, PA: Harper and Rowe.

Webster, L. (Ed.). (1989). *Sexual assault and child sexual assault: A national directory of victim/survivor services and prevention programs.* Phoenix, AZ: Oryx Press.

Weis, K. & Borges, S.S. (1973). "Victimology and rape: The ease of the legitimate victim," *Issues in Criminology,* 8, 71-115.

Willmarth, M. (1985). *Not for women only! A rape awareness program for men.* Presented at the American College Personnel Association (ACPA) National Conference, Boston, MA.

Wilson, J.Q. & Kelling, G.L. (1989). *Broken windows.* In R.G. Dunham & G.P. Alpert (Eds.). *Critical issues in policing: Contemporary readings.* Prospect Heights, IL: Waveland Press Inc.

Witt, P.H. (1988). "Psychological aspects of rapists," *New Jersey Trial Lawyer,* 1, (4), 67-70.

Zehner, M. (1981). "Emotional reactions to acquaintance rape," *WOARPATH,* 7, (11), 3.